THE SOCIOLOGIST'S STATISTICAL TOOLS

Computer Based Data Analysis Using SPSS *Windows*

Henry W. Fischer, III

University Press of America, Inc.
Lanham • New York • London

Copyright © 1996 by
University Press of America,® Inc.
4720 Boston Way
Lanham, Maryland 20706

3 Henrietta Street
London, WC2E 8LU England

Library of Congress Cataloging-in-Publication Data

Fischer, Henry
The sociologist's statistical tools : computer based data analysis using
SPSS Windows / Henry W. Fischer III.
p.   cm.
Includes bibliographical references and index.
1. Sociology--Statistical methods--Computer programs. 2. SPSS for
Windows. I. Title.
HM48.F55   1996   300'.285'5369 --dc20   96-15788 CIP

ISBN 0-7618-0356-4 (cloth: alk. ppr.)
ISBN 0-7618-0357-2 (pbk: alk. ppr.)

DEDICATED TO

Betsy and Jennifer,

Both of Whom I am Very Proud

CONTENTS

FOREWORD

Few skills are as important in sociology as statistics. At the same time few skills are more feared. The lore around undergraduate education in statistics is littered with stories of endless calculations, obtuse presentations and countless "blank stares" as students try to make sense of the "numbers." Some of this fear is based on poor student preparation, but academics must accept the fact that the presentation of statistics in sociology probably lacks three important things. First, it doesn't fully integrate modern technology into teaching and learning statistics. Secondly, it doesn't emphasize the relevance of statistics to sociology. Third, and finally, it lacks passion. Henry Fischer's *The Sociologist's Statistical Tools: Computer Based Data Analysis Using SPSS Windows* is a book that attempts to address all three. Let's take them in turn.

Integrates Modern Technology into Teaching and Learning Statistics

The emphasis in teaching social statistics has shifted from calculation of statistics to selection of the right statistics. Knowing "which statistic to use and when to use it" and, then, how to calculate it has always been important. However, truly understanding when the correct statistical technique is used is often lost in "battling" the calculations.

While few instructors would disagree that students must learn to choose and calculate statistics, students are increasingly surrounded by computer software which make calculations effortless so that they may spend more time on statistical selection. Henry Fischer's work integrates one of the most commonly available software packages, SPSS, into the presentation of statistics. The steps in using SPSS are laid out in a clear, understandable, "cookbook" arrangement. Fischer has minimized the "calculation and software wars!" This allows a student to spend more time on the logic of the match between the sociological problem at hand and the statistics required to help solve it.

Emphasize the Relevance of Statistics to Sociology

"Why do we have to do this? I took sociology because I'm interested in people!" This is a common and legitimate concern voiced by many undergraduates who realized that a statistics course is a requirement for their sociology program. The concerns for relevance to sociology and the personal value to students are both appropriate issues for any statistics book to be a credible tool. Henry Fischer addresses both of these. First, by using SPSS, students automatically gain exposure to a relevant software package. Programming SPSS is a relevant skill that students will need across a wide spectrum of disciplines not the least of which is sociology. Secondly, the data sets and problems used in this book bring students face-to-face with applied and basic research issues. The work provides an excellent first experience with statistics and the research process.

Passion for Statistics . . . and Sociology

Let's face it, statistics could be the most boring subject on the face of the planet! Even if its presentation is relevant and uses modern software, some students . . . and, often some instructors . . . find it difficult to show much enthusiasm for the subject. As Henry Fischer says, he "loves this stuff!" Students may still wonder why they should get excited if some "numbers geek" is thrilled over statistics, but Fischer's excitement can't help but rub off. "He'll get you!" You had better watch out or you may get excited about statistics too!

This book has all the pieces of a true adventure in sociology: passion, relevance and good solid skills. Students should beware Fischer's excitement is contagious . . . you might even end up liking and effectively using statistics!

Stephen F. Steele
Past-President, Society for Applied Sociology
Anne Arundel Community College
February 1996

PREFACE

Long after most of you would go home for the day, and long after I could have done the same, I am sitting here at my word processor preparing this draft of my manuscript which is designed to help you master the tools (computers and statistics) which sociologists use to have fun analyzing data, to look for behavior patterns and to seek answers to their research questions. Some sort of deadline, brought on by procrastination, is not the reason why I am sitting here letting my fingers do the talking. I love this stuff; this is one of my hobbies. You may think I am crazy, but I look forward to those times when I can come into my office, turn on my music, and compose my prose or run my data. It is my goal to help you through a semester during which you will learn the basics of data analysis. It is my goal to help you find the same joy that I have found in this enterprise. You will learn how to use the computer, how to use SPSS Windows, how to determine which statistics are needed for data analysis, how to interpret them, and how to write a report which presents your findings in answer to a research question.

I have heard for the last two decades that there are two types of people in the world: those who love computers and those who hate them. This may be true. In most of my statistics and research methods classes I have had what seems to be members of each of these two groups, despite my enthusiasm and superior teaching skills (yes, you can chuckle-- I am trying to be light hearted). There may also be several subgroups of computer users. There are those who enjoy using word processing programs to write their papers, those who use statistical packages for data analysis, those who seek information on the Web, those who enjoy computer conferencing or chatrooms, and those who enjoy several or all of these things. I fall into the later category. You may fall into any of these . . . or, perhaps, you may decide that the computer is not user friendly for you-- but I doubt that!

I have high hopes for each and every student who uses this book. You see, I may now sound like a fanatic to you, but I can assure you that this has not always been the case. I once sat where you do now. When I was an undergraduate I did not see myself as a likely candidate to fall in love with the computer and it's varied software options. If my stats prof had told me that I would return as a prof myself and become a bit of a computer jock, I would have never believed it. In fact, I would have considered it a safe bet to offer my future lifetime earnings with a thousand-to-one odds against it. But here I am! And, for better or worse, so are you. I hope to sow some seeds of hope that may result in your future being similar to mine, at least in enthusiasm. So, let's get going and find out what you have gotten yourself into by majoring in Sociology and, thereby, agreeing to take this course.

Math Statistics Recommended As a Pre-Requisite

This book is not expected to replace a mathematics exposure to statistics. It is written to facilitate student mastery of statistics and computer skills commonly needed for the undergraduate sociology student. In short, this book is written to help the sociology student become competent with statistics *as the user!* In my university we actually have a three semester sequence. First our students complete a course in math statistics, the traditional course which exposes students to what the computer will later do for them. The second course is the course you are now taking with the help of this book. We call it our Social Statistics course while other institutions often call the same course Data Analysis. The third course in our series is Research Methodology which is where the students learn how to design a research project. They conduct their own research project applying the skills learned in the Social Statistics or Data Analysis course.

Comments About Hands-On Experience and this Book

We do not all learn the same way. Some of us seem to thrive in the traditional lecture setting. I often lecture, but I prefer the hands-on approach for learning and using social statistics. For most of us experiential learning is fun. This course should be one in which you will be engaged in primarily experiential learning. A great deal of in-class and out-of-class time will necessarily be spent in the computer lab. Of course "fun" may be operationalized differently by each researcher. Attitude is everything! If you can catch some of my enthusiasm, you *will* enjoy learning how to make the computer help you numerically describe and explain social reality. Good luck, let's have fun. Time to start!

Special Message to Instructors

Codebooks and data have been provided in the appendix for student application activities. You may also wish to provide your own data or obtain commercially provided data sets, e.g., General Social Survey, Crime Victimization Studies. It is my hope that each of use will use "whatever works" for us and our students. Enjoy.

ACKNOWLEDGMENTS

An author is essentially the pen through which significant others write. There are so many who have contributed to leading me to being able to offer this work in the hopes of aiding students conquer the delightful territory we know as statistics and the research process. I am sure I will inadvertently overlook someone to whom I am indebted. I, therefore, want to first thank *them* and apologize for my inadequate memory.

Millersville University of Pennsylvania has provided me with released time to facilitate the writing process. I am grateful for the support of the Department of Sociology and Anthropology, the School of Humanities and Social Sciences, the Faculty Grants Committee, and the university.

I am grateful for the teaching and direction of those who contributed extensively to my graduate school training in statistics and research design. The faculty at the University of Delaware to whom I am indebted include Barry Morstain of the Department of Urban Affairs and all of the members of the Department of Sociology, especially Allan McCutcheon and Frank Scarpitti. I can never thank

them enough for what they have given to me, and in turn, to *my*
students!

A tremendous great of gratitude is also owed several others. I
thank Stephen Steele, past-president of the Society for Applied
Sociology and author of the foreword for this book. Steve continues
to be a role model for me during my career. He has provided me
with continual inspiration and support. I have met his delightful
students and I know I don't have to tell them how lucky they are to
have him--they already know! I also thank Carla Howery and the
American Sociological Association for granting me permission to use
some of my earlier work, *Social Statistics, the IBM\PC and
SPSS\PC+*, which they published in 1993 as part of the ASA's
Teaching Resources Series. Carla, the ASA, and the ASA journal,
Teaching Sociology, continually strive to contribute to quality teaching.
I also want to thank Kathleen McKinney and the rest of the staff of
the aforementioned ASA journal for their help in publishing my piece
in the April 1996 issue which describes Millersville University's
sociology research program.

I want to also thank all of my past, present, and future students.
This work is offered to you in the hope that it will make your passage
into data analysis easier and more enjoyable. I expect that some of
you will find that you have found your life's work through this
process. I tip my hat to you as you jump in with both feet and take
your skills as far as you can.

Last, but certainly not least, I want to thank my loving, supportive
family. I owe much to my wife, Donna, my daughters Betsy and
Jennifer, my parents and my parents-in-law.

CHAPTER 1

INTRODUCTION TO SOCIAL STATISTICS

Behavior! Isn't that what we are interested in? In fact, you were probably drawn to social science because of your interest in understanding people and their problems, right? Social scientists seek to describe, explain, and predict human behavior patterns. When we conduct research we are usually seeking to explain social reality through the gathering and interpreting of relevant data. How does the sociologist interpret this data? For example, when a sociologist administers a questionnaire to find out how many college students have been victims of crime, observes male-female interaction in order to determine if a patriarchy dominates their relationships, conducts a telephone interview to assess who is ahead in the race for President, devises an experiment to measure effective child-rearing techniques, or evaluates the effectiveness of a rehabilitation program for delinquent juveniles, how does she determine the answer to her research question? There are certain tools the researcher employs.

This book will teach you the basic tools the contemporary sociologist, criminologist, and anthropologist use. These tools include the descriptive and explanatory statistics commonly employed in data analysis and in the reporting of one's findings as well as the computer technology necessary to assess these findings. You will be trained how to use the basic statistical procedures, how to report your findings, and how to use *SPSS Windows* in order to obtain them.

What is SPSS? The Statistical Package for the Social Sciences (SPSS Windows) is one of the leading computer software programs designed to enable social researchers to analyze their data (other popular statistical packages include SAS and Minitab). It can tabulate the number of females and males in a study, calculate the average income of the respondents, compare income by gender, determine if there is a statistically significant difference between the income paid to men versus that paid to women, and so forth. SPSS can provide frequency distributions, crosstabulations, calculate descriptive statistics (mean, median, mode, range, interquartile range, standard deviation), as well as explanatory statistics (chi-square, Pearson correlation coefficients, multiple-regression, t-tests, and so forth).

While a course in social statistics can be based upon any statistical software appropriate to social research, this book is designed to facilitate learning and using our common statistical tools with the help of SPSS Windows. If after graduation you find yourself in a job which uses a different statistical package you should be able to easily apply what you have learned from this book and SPSS Windows to your situation. Each statistical package is simply a variation of the same statistical theme.

What Is This Thing Called "Statistics?" It is *not* a method for proving anything one wants to prove. It is not simply a collection of facts--there is no substitute for sound theoretical analysis. It is not something that is used only when there is a large number of people in the sample. It is not a substitute for interviewing or using other research methods (the data gathering tool must fit the problem being studied). "Statistics" include an array of tools designed to help *describe* the sample or population from which data was gathered and to *explain* the possible relationship(s) between two or more variables. There are essentially two types of statistics: *descriptive statistics* which help us describe those studied (percentages, means, medians, modes, range, standard deviations) and *explanatory statistics* which help us determine if two or more variables influence one another (chi-square, t-test, ANOVA, linear correlation and regression, multiple regression).

If you want to know how many females and males were in your sample and if you also want to know if the men earned significantly more than the women, both descriptive and explanatory statistics would be helpful. For example, percentages help you describe the gender composition of the sample when you find that a majority (52%) of the sample were female (48% being male). You use the mean to determine the average salary earned last year by the females and males in the sample. And, you might use the t-test to determine if the gender difference in salary is statistically significant.

Of course, as a researcher you would also want to investigate the various reasons for the observed salary difference, e.g., years of work experience may vary by gender, educational level might vary by gender, and so forth. SPSS could be used to *control* for these variables, i.e., compare only those men and women with similar work experience or similar educational backgrounds, and, thereby, determine if it is indeed these variations in work and educational experience that explain salary differences-- or, if gender alone explains the observed difference. The social statistics presented in this book are useful tools which help us to describe and explain what is happening in the real social world we seek to investigate and understand.

The Place of Statistics in the Research Process. I want to leave you with a few words of advice. Do not be awed by statistics or by statisticians. Statistics are useful tools in the hands of the individual who knows what she is doing. The importance of statistics in the research process is sometimes exaggerated, however. The numbers *never* speak for themselves and *never prove* anything. These tools help us determine how reliable our data is, how representative we can expect our sample to be, and how strongly two or more variables are associated with one another. In the end *we* must interpret the meaning of the numbers. This decision must be based upon our knowledge of statistics and the sociological perspective. While statistics are actually computed during the analysis stage of a research project, after the data is gathered, cleaned and entered into the computer, one must consider which statistical procedures are relevant when designing a research project. Statistical analysis cannot compensate for a poor research design or poorly gathered data. Remember, they are only tools! Having made this point, I do not want to suggest that the statistician is not a skilled individual undeserving of respect. I just want to make sure you know the limits of statistics and their proper role.

Using Examples to Reduce Anxiety. Just in case you have been suffering from some anxiety in approaching this course, let's look at a few examples of how statistics are used to describe behavior--using one statistic you are very familiar with already, percentages. Use the percentages you see below to describe the people being studied, at least with respect to their gender composition.

Gender
(N=854)

Females	52%
Males	48%
	100%

There were a total of 854 respondents in this study. The sample was composed of slightly more females (52%) than males (48%). The statistic known as the percentage is used every day to describe the makeup of a group.

Let's look at another example. Use percentages and the other statistical information provided to describe the respondents.

Age
(N=854)

18 - 34	23%
35 - 49	32%
50 - 59	25%
60 +	20%
	100%

Mean = 37   Median = 35

Okay, what do we have? Approximately a fourth of the sample are young adults, i.e., between 18 and 34 years of age (23%). Almost a third (32%) are between the ages of 35 and 49 while a fourth (25%) are well into middle age, between 50 and 59. The remaining respondents (20%) are older Americans, i.e., over 60. There appear to be more middle-aged people than any other age group if we combine the 35-59 year-olds and define this as middle-age. The average respondent is 37 and half of these people are below, and half are above, 35 years of age. . . .

We've just used three types of basic descriptive statistics to describe our sample: percentages, mean, and median. Does it get any harder than this. Well, yes but not by very much. We will use other types of descriptive statistics and we will learn to use explanatory statistics such as chi-square, t-tests, ANOVA, correlation coefficients, and multiple regression. When you get used to them, however, you will find them to be easy to use. Statistics are fun to use because they help us describe and explain behavior patterns. As sociologists, criminologists, and anthropologists isn't this what we are all about?

Let's try one more. Look at the next table and describe what you see here. Can you also hypothesize why this is happening?

		Gender	
		Female	Male
Abuse Spouse?	Yes	8%	32%
	No	92%	68%
		100%	100%
		(345)	(332)

Chi-Square = 34.56   df = 1   Significance = .05

Did you observe that men in this sample are far more likely to have been abusive toward their spouse than women? Almost all of the women (92%) have reportedly not been abusive, while a third (32%) of the men have been. Furthermore, as you will soon learn, according to the chi-square test results, this difference is a statistically significant one. In the current study, men are more likely to have been abusive than women. Can you hypothesize why this may be so? Gender role socialization anyone? Men may continue to be socialized to be aggressive while women, on the other hand, may continue to be socialized to be more passive. If domestic violence had been observed in one's family of orientation, one may act abusively regardless of gender.

What I am trying to demonstrate is just how much fun the data analysis process can be. I hope I am succeeding in convincing you that it is fun. It is a hobby on mine--it can be one of yours as well. This process is the natural extension of the desire to understand human behavior, which drew us to social science in the first place. The post-modern information producing and consuming society we currently find ourselves in will increasingly reward those who do enjoy and undertake the process of creating, accessing, and interpreting human behavior patterns. We are probably on the threshold of a new, greater understanding of human behavior and the origins of the social problems generated by our social structures. The skills you gain in this course should help position you to be an active player in this new world of understanding. The future awaits those who embrace it.

The Use of Statistics in Reporting Findings

I don't know about you, but before I embark on a new journey I like to know what my destination is. When entering into a new classroom experience I think it is a good idea to see an example of what we are aiming to achieve. By having a model of the final product, you can compare what you are doing and learning in class to where it fits into the final product. So, at this juncture I provide my students with copies of examples of the various ways we report the findings of our data analysis. I usually provide my students with a copy of each of the following: (1) an "in-house report," i.e., a department self-study report prepared by our own Sociology and Anthropology Department, (2) a research contract final report, i.e., a final report prepared for the Commonwealth of Pennsylvania assessing earthquake preparedness, (3) a research paper presented at a national sociology conference, and (4) a journal article. The student should be able to see that in some respects each type of report is similar, yet different in key areas. For example, the more formal the research audience, it is likely the more sophisticated explanatory statistics will be used, e.g., multiple regression, while a simple in-house report or report prepared for a lay audience is more likely to simply use descriptive statistics. While some types of reports will not include a formal literature review, all reporting formats include some statement of what the research question or goal was, how the data was gathered, what was found and the meaning of these findings.

Courses in social statistics traditionally prepare students to be able to use the entire array of statistical procedures and train students to write formal research reports. Ultimately, every professor desires the student to be prepared for any form of reporting using the appropriate type and level of statistical analysis. The current text will outline the basic components of the traditional research report. You will be expected to model your reporting after this model. However, please remember that there are variations of this reporting model and you must consider your audience when preparing a presentation of your findings. The good data analyst is the one who presents her findings to an audience in the appropriate manner.

Basic Components of the Research Report

As you have undoubtedly observed, there are several required components that must be included in a research report. The five basic components of the report are the statement of the research question or problem, a review of the relevant sociological literature, a description of the methodology used to gather the data, a presentation of the findings and an explanation of the conclusions drawn from these findings. There are several additional items which also frame the basic contents of the report. These additional items include a title page, an abstract, a list of cited references, and an appendix which may include an array of items such as a copy of the questionnaire used to gather the data and the data tables cited in the findings section. The order in which these research report components appear follows:

Research Report Title Page
Abstract

* Statement of the Research Problem or Question
* Literature Review
* Methodology
* Findings
* Conclusions

Cited References
Appendices
       Tables
       Questionnaire

* denotes the five major components of a research report

Let's now briefly examine what is included in each of the report sections.

Research Report Title Page. A title is created which captures the essence of the research question. The author's name(s), institutional affiliation, and completion date are also usually included on the title page. If funding was provided to support the research, the granting agency is also identified. If the report is a paper to be presented at a professional meeting, then the organization, city and meeting date are included as well. Examine the examples your professor provided or search your library or the World Wide Web for examples.

Abstract.   The abstract is a brief statement summarizing the research question, its relevance to the literature, the primary data gathering method, as well as key findings and conclusions.   The abstract is normally no more than one single-spaced page. It is often no longer than 100-150 words.

Statement of the Research Question or Problem. This is the first major component of the report. It is the introduction to the research project. This section gives the reader a brief overview of what was researched and why it was important to do so-- how the findings would contribute to the existing research literature, to theory development, as well as how it may contribute to improving our society. The length of this introduction varies greatly. It is usually one to three pages long.

Literature Review.   The literature review accomplishes several tasks. First, it demonstrates to the reader that the researcher has a thorough understanding of the relevant issues gleaned from the existing research findings. Secondly, it establishes the relevance of the current work, i.e., building a case which demonstrates that the current research question is the next logical extension of the on-going work being conducted in the substantive research area under consideration. In other words, it identifies all of the relevant issues or variables the literature and the researcher consider germane to the current study.

Research Methodology.   The Methodology section describes, in detail, the research methods employed in conducting the project, e.g., how a mail questionnaire was used and how the sample was selected. It identifies the population from which the sample was drawn, the response rate, what was done to maximize the response rate, and what limitations result from the sampling procedures and the methodology employed.   This is also where variables are operationalized and where a description of measurement techniques appears. If hypotheses were developed and tested, a discussion and presentation of them is included this section of the report.

Findings.   There are two major sub-categories.   First, the researcher is expected to demographically describe the sample, e.g., makeup by gender, age, income, education, and so forth. The reader will thus obtain a picture of the respondents upon whom the findings are based. The second sub-category of the findings section is devoted to the substantive findings, i.e., a discussion of the tabulations of how the respondents answered the relevant interview questions and a presentation of the relevant data which contributes to answering the research question. Included in this section are relevant applications of variable means, standard deviations, chi-square test results, correlation coefficients, multiple regression, ANOVA, and t-test results.

It should be noted that much social research utilizes nothing more than frequency distributions, descriptive statistics, and elementary crosstabulations, e.g., comparing gender's possible influence on income. Some of us also use chi-square, correlation coefficients, multiple regression analysis, ANOVA and t-tests--but only when it makes sense to do so. The good researcher does not use every statistical procedure in the book just because these tools exist. The good researcher wisely selects those which are most appropriate to the task at hand.

Conclusions. In this section of the report, the researcher summarizes key findings, interprets their meaning, and, when possible, applies a sociological paradigm to add greater clarity to the interpretation of the findings. She may also discuss their practical application, make suggestions for future research, note the limitations of the present findings, and indicate any methodological implications discovered during the project.

Cited References. The American Sociological Association format is followed when providing the bibliographic details of the cited references. ASA format essentially means alphabetically listing references, last name, followed by first. The date of the publication is next, followed by the title, city and publisher. In the case of a journal article the references substitute the name of the journal for the publisher, excludes city, and also adds the issue number and page numbers. The ASA formats for a book and a journal article follow.

Book Format:

Fischer, Henry W., III. 1994. *Response to Disaster: Fact Versus Fiction & Its Perpetuation.* Lanham, Maryland: University Press of America.

Journal Format:

Fischer, Henry W., III and Marna L. Trowbridge. 1992.
"The Limited Role of Disaster Experience in Mitigation
Adjustment." *Disaster Management* 4-3:131-137.

Appendix. Tables are listed in the Appendix. They should be
numbered consecutively, in the order in which they are referred to in
the text. For example, Table 1 should include frequency distributions
for the demographic variables. Table 2 should include frequency
distributions for the substantive variables and Table 3 should include
the crosstabulations which compare independent and dependent
variables for possible relationships. A copy of the data gathering tool
should also be included in the Appendix. For example, whether you
used a mail-questionnaire, an observation guide, or a content analysis
form, include a copy in the Appendix.

Levels of Measurement

In most research projects one is working within a theoretical
framework, e.g., structural-functionalist, conflict theory, symbolic
interactionist, feminist. A research question is crafted from within
the chosen theoretical perspective, the relevant literature is reviewed,
and hypotheses may be designed for testing. Before the researcher
decides the best way to gather the needed data and which statistical
procedures are appropriate for testing the hypotheses, she must
decide how to define, in a measurable way, the variables used in the
study. All variables, e.g., demographic, substantive, independent and
the dependent variables, must be operationally defined. For example,
let's work with the following hypothesis:

*The higher the Socio-Economic Status (SES) of the individual,
the lower the observed degree of racial prejudice.*

SES is the independent variable (I, or what we think is the cause) and
prejudice is the dependent variable (D, or what we think is the
effect). How can we measure these two variables in order to
determine if the hypothesis is true? We must *define the* variables so
they can be measured and compared. We may decide to use the
following income levels to define low, moderate and high SES (our
"definition" must make good sociological sense, however, it cannot be
arbitrary):

Socio-Economic Status

high:	yearly family income of $100,000 or more
moderate:	$30,000 to $99,999
low:	$29,999 or less

And, we may have developed a test to assess the extent to which the respondent is prejudiced. Perhaps we designed a series of 50 questions to which the respondent agrees or disagrees. The completely unprejudiced individual would disagree with each statement and earn no points, while the completely prejudiced individual could earn a maximum score of 50 after agreeing with each prejudiced statement. If this scaled test is a good sociological assessment of degree of prejudice we might find the following operational definition appropriate:

Prejudice

high:	scoring 40 to 50 on the study's prejudice scale
moderate:	scoring 20 to 39
low:	scoring 19 or less

By defining variables in an observable, measurable way, we can determine if an *increase* in SES is accompanied with a corresponding *decrease* in observed racial prejudice.

When the researcher operationally defines variables, she may be working at what we call different levels of measurement because not all variables have equal numerical properties. Hence, they cannot be utilized in our computations in the same fashion. Some variables are nominal level or sweatshirt variables, some are ordinal level variables, while others are interval level (or interval-ratio) variables.

Nominal. A nominal variable is one in which the number you assign to the variable categories merely serves as a code for identifying that person. A good analogy is the numbering system for sweatshirts in football or field hockey. A football lineman who plays tackle is usually numbered in the 70's (like 72 or 77). This number on his sweatshirt only means he plays tackle, it is not a reflection of how well he plays the position or how much money he is paid. Gender is a nominal variable. We may ask the following on a questionnaire:

What sex are you?
    (1) female
    (2) male

Being male (answer number 2) is not twice as good as being female (does one male equal two females?). We could just as easily, and just as accurately, ask the question this way:

What sex are you?
    (1) male
    (2) female

Reversing the numerical order in a nominal variable does not change the interpretation of what the numbers mean. The numbers are mere codes for identification purposes. It does not matter what number you name or assign a male versus a female respondent.

Ordinal. In the case of the ordinal variable, order *is* important. Change the order of how you number the answers and you change the meaning. If we ask:

Approximately how much money did you earn last year? ____

and if we then categorize the salaries of the various survey respondents into the following categories:

Income
    (1) low income
    (2) moderate income
    (3) upper income

the order of how we number the answer options *does* matter. As we move from answer 1 to answer 2 and then to answer 3, we find that we are moving from a lower to an increasingly (in order) higher level of income. The number 1 connotes less than answer number 2, and 2 is expected to be less than 3. The order is important. If we changed the ordering to:

Income
    (1) moderate income
    (2) upper income
    (3) lower income

then we have changed what it means to move from answer 1 to 2 to 3. There is no order from low to high (1 being normally associated with the low value and 3 with the higher value). This answer sequence makes no sense!

Education is a good example of a variable which often appears as an ordinal variable on a questionnaire. For example:

How much formal education have you completed?
__ 1. less than high school
__ 2. high school graduate
__ 3. college

Interval. Interval level variables are those which not only have order but which also are measured with separate, numerical, measured intervals, and usually have a meaning of their own beyond the coding process of the study. For example, a respondent could be asked to state her exact income:

What was your total family income last year? ___

In this instance we would end up with interval level data which consists of the exact income. The interval between each salary might be one dollar, e.g., respondent 1 earned $33,000, respondent 2 earned $33,001 and respondent 3 earned $33,002. More likely, the respondents would have salaries scattered across the spectrum of possibilities such as: $18,000, $22,500, $28,000, $75,850. The implied interval is, never-the-less, one dollar.

Interval level data is often grouped, however. For example, respondents are often asked in check the category which most closely corresponds to their salary:

What was your total family income last year?

__ 1. $20k or less
__ 2. $21k - $40k
__ 3. $41k - $60k
__ 4. $61k +

Now the intervals are $20,000 each. In the first example of interval level data, the numbers (the actual salaries) are not codes. The salaries had meaning in themselves. In the second example of interval level data, the numbers are once again codes: "1" represents "$20,000 or less" per year, and so forth. But the numbers have order and each number represents an equal interval, in this case, of $20,000 each.

Ungrouped interval level data could be grouped or categorized, of course. You could recode respondents into grouped intervals. You could also recode them into categories such as "low income," "moderate income," or "upper income" which could entail unequal intervals, then the codes ("1," "2," and "3") represent a change in the data from interval level into ordinal level. It is sometimes desireable to recode in this manner. It is generally better to obtain interval level data when it is possible to do so and then recode it into ordinal or nominal level variables if it is prudent to do so. If you only obtain income data in nominal or ordinal form, you cannot then recode it into interval level. Some statistical procedures can only be used with interval level data. The rule of thumb is select the appropriate level of measure for your study, but strive to obtain the highest level of data (interval or ordinal versus nominal) possible. You will latter learn which statistical tests are appropriate for which levels of measurement.

APPLICATION QUESTIONS

1. Examine the contents of a journal article, professional paper or research report. Indicate whether or not all of the basic components of a research report are present. Identify the basic research question, the primary independent and dependent variables, the level of measurement used for each of these variables (i.e., indicate whether each is nominal, ordinal, or interval level), and the types of statistics that are used. Summarize, in your own words, the findings and conclusions.

2. Create three hypotheses of your own. Identify the independent and dependent variable for each & operationally define each variable.

3. Examine a copy of the codebook for the General Social Survey (or an alternative similar resource such as a codebook for the U.S. Bureau of Criminal Justice Crime Victimization Study). Select three variables from the codebook: one nominal level variable, one ordinal, and two interval level variables (one ungrouped and one grouped).

4. Larry told a classmate that he had completed his data analysis over the weekend. "I proved that juvenile rehab bootcamp programs don't work to prevent recidivism." If you were Larry's classmate, how would you respond to his findings?

LAB SESSION

Session I:1

1. Go to the computer lab and format two separate disks so that you can keep copies of important data files and reports in case one disk gets damaged.

2. Access the Web and determine if your library has any of the following:

Books

Etzioni, Amitai. 1993. *The Spirit of Community. Rights, Responsibilities, and the Communitarian Agenda.* New York: Crown Publishers, Inc.

Fischer, Henry W., III. 1994. *Response to Disaster: Fact Versus Fiction & Its Perpetuation. The Sociology of Disaster.* Lanham, Maryland: University Press of America.

West, Cornel. 1993. *Race Matters.* New York: Vintage.

Article

Fischer, Henry W., III. 1996. "Teaching Statistics From the User's Perspective." *Teaching Sociology* 24:225-230.

3. E-mail your professor a message to report on which of the above are in your library.

CHAPTER 2

GETTING STARTED

When do you use the computer? My answer is always. Remember I am a true believer! Perhaps I should elaborate. When do we use the statistical and computing tools available to us? The answer is simple; we use them whenever we are gathering data to answer a research question. If you distribute a questionnaire, conduct some face-to-face or telephone interviews, complete a content analysis, carry out an experiment, quantify some data gathered during field work, and so forth, you will want to use *SPSS Windows* to tabulate and describe your findings as well as determine if any statistically significant relationships are observable in your data.

The process is really a simple one and it is fun. You start by creating a codebook to help you remember what you named your variables and how you coded the answer options, e.g., perhaps you coded females as category "1" and males as category "2." Next you use SPSS to enter your raw data into a data file which will look like a spreadsheet. And finally you simply tell the computer to tabulate the answers to your questionnaire questions (or interview questions, etc.) in order to help you describe the respondents and their answers (for example, their *average* age and *median* income). You also us the computer to help you compare the variables which you think may be related to one another (for example, does more formal education lead to higher starting salaries--you hope so!).

Chapter 2 of this book will train you to create a codebook and a data file so that, with the help of Chapter 3, you will be able to begin data analysis. Let's work with a specific illustration. Let's say you have a questionnaire you distributed to a sample of students on campus. You are interested in determining if alcohol consumption increases among students as they progress through the student subculture, i.e., rise from the status of the poor lowly freshman to that of the exhaulted senior. Please refer to the *Student Alcohol Survey* found in Illustration II:1.

Each question represents a separate variable for which information is obtained. The first three variables in this illustration, sex, age, and status, are commonly referred to as *demographic variables* as they help the researcher describe the demographic makeup of the respondents, i.e., gender composition, age range and average age, and the status composition (primarily underclassmen, upperclassmen or combination of each). These demographic variables may also be treated as possible *independent* variables as well. We usually automatically test to see if any are. Often they tend to be poor predictors of behavior, i.e., they turn out to **not** be independent variables, but sometimes they are associated with variation in the behavior under study. In other words, sometimes being male may be found to be associated with consuming larger amounts of alcohol than females. The last two variables in Illustration II:1 are considered to be *substantive* variables. The frequency with which one goes out to drink and the amount consumed during a drinking episode are the variables designed to examine the substance of the research question (drinking behavior patterns). In this case they are also considered to be the *dependent* variables, at least we are going to test to see if they are.

When conducting actual research, the sociologist would normally be gathering data on many more variables than these few. Most of the substantive variables would actually be independent variables, not dependent. So, please do not assume that this brief illustration is identical to most research projects. Also, we normally place the questions requesting demographic information at the *end of the questionnaire*.

Let's take a closer look at the variables in this illustration. We have one nominal variable which is the gender of the respondent, we have one interval variable which is the age of the respondent, and we

Illustration II:1

Student Alcohol Survey

Dear Respondents:

We are conducting a survey to better understand student drinking patterns. Your cooperation in this study will be greatly appreciated. If you choose to participate, please indicate the answer that best describes your experiences by placing an "X" on the line beside the most appropriate answer to each question. Thank you very much in anticipation of your help.

A. First we'd like to ask a few questions to help us analyze the results of the study.

    1. What is your sex?
        — (a) female
        — (b) male

    2. What is your current age (in years)? ____

    3. Based upon completed credits, what is your current student status?
        — (a) freshman
        — (b) sophomore
        — (c) junior
        — (d) senior
        — (e) graduate student

B. Now we'd like to ask a few questions about your drinking experiences.

    4. During an average semester, how often do you drink a beverage which contains alcohol (beer, wine, or liquor)?
        — (a) never
        — (b) once or twice a semester
        — (c) once a month
        — (d) several times a month
        — (e) weekly
        — (f) several times a week
        — (g) daily
        — (h) several times a day

    5. During a typical sitting, how much do you consume?
        — (a) none
        — (b) one serving (can or glass)
        — (c) two or three servings
        — (d) four to six servings
        — (e) seven to ten servings
        — (f) more than ten servings

have three ordinal variables--the status, drinking frequency and amount usually consumed in a single sitting. Each variable is operationally defined in a measurable way except for age which is implied (21 will mean twenty-one years of age and so forth).

The well organized researcher will not only create the data gathering tool, in this illustration the questionnaire, but will also create the codebook and data file prior to beginning the data gathering process. As the questionnaires are being completed and returned to the researcher, she can head to the computer lab and enter the raw data into the previously created data file. This procedure avoids being swamped with 200 questionnaires all at once. It is allot easier to enter 30 questionnaires worth of information at a time.

Creating the Codebook

In preparation for data entry the researcher prepares a codebook which identifies the variables by name (a variable name is limited to ten characters), a short statement clarifying the meaning of variable name (for example, "Sex" means "the gender of the respondent"), and the code and label for each answer category (for example, "1" means "female" and "2" means "male") for each variable (for each questionnaire question). The codebook should be wordprocessed and several copies should be printed. The researcher not only uses the codebook to help create the data file and enter data into it, but whenever she seeks to do data analysis the codebook will be referred to as a memory aid. You may forget whether you called the first question in our illustration "sex" or "gender" and you may forget if your answers listed "female" first (as a coded "1") or second (as a coded "2"). Refer to Illustration II:2 for an example of a codebook for our sample questionnaire.

In our sample codebook there are five variables each of which corresponds to the question in the questionnaire. The nominal (sex) and ordinal (status, freq, amount) variables have their answer categories designated by numerical codes. The ungrouped interval level variable (age) does not need such coding as the number provided by the respondent has meaning in its own right, e.g., "21" means twenty-one years of age, "35" means thirty-five years of age, we don't have to code and label each age value. If age had been a grouped interval level variable, i.e., if we had offered respondents categories of ages to check [(1) Under 21, (2) 21-25, (3) 26-35, (4) 36-45, and so forth], then we would have to offer codes and labels for those codes in our codebook. Compare our sample codebook with

Illustration II:2

Codebook for Student Alcohol Survey

1. SEX   Gender of the Respondent
(1) female
(2) male

2. AGE   Age of the Respondent (given in years)

3. STATUS   Status in College Based on Completed Credits
(1) freshman
(2) sophomore
(3) junior
(4) senior
(5) graduate student

4. FREQ   Drinking Frequency Per Semester
(1) never
(2) 1-2 sem
(3) 1 mon
(4) sev per mon
(5) weekly
(6) sev per wk
(7) daily
(8) sev per day

5. AMOUNT   Drinking Amount Per Episode
(1) none
(2) 1 serving
(3) 2-3 servings
(4) 4-6 servings
(5) 7-10 servings
(6) 10+ servings

the sample questionnaire.

The codebook should be an abbreviated version of the questionnaire. After creating, proof reading and printing copies of the codebook the researcher is ready to head to the lab. It's now time to create the data file.

Preparing for Data Analysis

How will you learn to create a data file and use *SPSS Windows*? This book should help a great deal, but a key source of your learning will be your instructor who will show you how to do everything presented in this book. He or she will lead you through the learning process in the computer lab. SPSS, Inc., publishes a reference manual, the current publication as of this writing is *SPSS for Windows--Base System and SPSS 6.1 and 7.0 for Windows Updates*. You can normally find a copy of the current publication in most computer labs. This publication will be very helpful in answering detailed questions about how to use SPSS. Many instructors also require their students to buy a copy of this publication in addition to the textbook they use for their course. Another excellent source is the *SPSS Tutorial*. Labs that have *SPSS Windows* also have the tutorial program on their computers. This tutorial is what I call "dummy proof." All you have to do is access the program and do what it tells you to do and you will learn the basics in how to create a data file, as well as everything else you will learn in this course. The tutorial program is a good adjunct to your course instructor. Let's give it a try.

Using the Tutorial. When you are in the Windows environment, use the mouse to select (point and click twice) the SPSS package icon. You will find several SPSS package options, each with their own icon. For example, you will see the SPSS program icon, the Sample Data icon, and the SPSS Tutorial program icon. Select the latter. When you enter the tutorial the first master menu will appear on your monitor listing eight program options. Illustration II:3 lists these eight options. Begin by selecting "How to Use the Tutorial," I told you it was dummy proof. This option will explain how to navigate around the tutorial program itself.

Select "Overview" next. This option will give you an overview of how SPSS works, i.e., helping you create a data file, conduct data analysis, and obtain output (tables, charts, graphs). After finishing the overview, you should select "Getting Data Into SPSS" (I suggest that you don't use any of the other five options in the tutorial at this time. By using the first three you will be exposed to everything you need to know at this time. More might result in overload!). This third tutorial option will lead you through the steps pursuant to opening, creating, and saving your raw questionnaire data in an SPSS data file.

Illustration II:3

SPSS Tutorial Main Menu

HOW TO USE THE TUTORIAL	CREATING CHARTS
OVERVIEW	MODIFYING CHARTS
GETTING DATA INTO SPSS	SAVING YOUR WORK
ANALYZING DATA	GETTING HELP

Creating An SPSS Data File. [Before you go any further, make sure you have an appropriate disk available and formatted--ask your instructor how to format your disk if you don't already know how.] From the Windows environment, select the SPSS icon. An empty spreadsheet should appear on your monitor. To open a new file, select "File" from the menu box (see the tutorial and/or SPSS manual for an explanation of the menu box and tool box as well as any other SPSS vocabulary that is unfamiliar to you in this text). After selecting "File" from the menu box, a list of menu options will appear, select "New" and then, in the additional menu box which appears, select "Data." Illustration II:4 will provide you with an abbreviated list of all the steps for creating a data file.

Labeling Variables & Answer Values. Working with your codebook as a guide, use the first column of the spreadsheet for your first variable (unless you decide to use ID Codes in column 1, ask your instructor about this option). With the cursor over the first column, click the mouse twice, a dialogue box will then appear. Type in the name of the first variable, e.g., "Sex." Next you want access the variable label option and type the label for the first variable, e.g., "Gender of Respondent." Now you will enter the codes and labels for the answer options for the first variable, e.g., "1" as "female" and "2" as "male." Select "Add" after completing these steps, then select "Continue" and "OK." You will return to the spreadsheet and the name of your first variable will appear at the top of column 1. Proceed in similar fashion for all the remaining variables until you are done naming each column (along with the variable and value labels), i.e., variable.

Entering Data. Now that you have labeled all your variables and their respective values (answer options, e.g., "1" for "female" and "2" for male, and so forth), you are ready to begin entering the actual responses of each respondent, i.e., the raw data. With the cursor in the first column and first row (e.g., column for Sex, row for respondent 1), click once and the box will become highlighted as your work area. Type the value for the respondent's answer, e.g., if this respondent is a female you would type "1" and then click the mouse again (or hit the enter key). The "1" should now be located in your first column, first row. Click the box for the second variable of the first respondent. Type the code for this answer, click the mouse, and so forth, until every answer for respondent number 1 is entered into the spreadsheet. You are then ready to enter the data for respondent 2 through respondent "n."

Saving the Data File. After entering your data, you will need to save it. Select "File," then select "Save Data As," select proper disk drive ("a:" if your want to save the data on your own disk), then name your file and click "OK." The name you give your data file must end in ".SAV" while *you* may decide what to use as a prefix. For example, if you are doing a crime study, why not name your data file "CRIME.SAV"? Of course, you also need the disk destination, e.g., "a:\CRIME.SAV" before you can click "OK." Your data file will be saved on your disk under the chosen name--its very own address.

Re-Entering an Existing Data File. When you want to get back into your data file to continue working (to add more data or begin data analysis), select "File," select "Open," select "Data," select the disk the file is on (e.g., "a:"), select the named file you want to work with (e.g., "a:\crime.sav"), and finally select "OK." The selected data file will appear in the spreadsheet on your monitor. You are ready to go to work adding more data, recoding existing data (to be discussed later), or begin data analysis.

After adding more data to the data file, you must re-save the data file to include this additional information on your disk. Select "File," then select "Save" in order to save your new data. Do this every time you make changes to your data file.

Accessing Data Files on the Server. The computers in most labs are connected to a server which provides common access to data files for anyone working in the lab. To access any data files on the server, select "File," select "Open," select "Data," select the server (e.g., "s:") as the "disk" (rather than "a:") from which you will then select the name of the file you want to bring up to the spreadsheet.

Obtaining a Printed Hard Copy of Your Spreadsheet. It's always a good idea to obtain a printed hard copy of your data file to help you compare what you entered into the spreadsheet with the actual data on your questionnaires. You must always double, if not triple, check to make sure data entry is correct. Mistakes are too easily made and your conclusions would then be based upon incorrect information. With the spreadsheet on your monitor, select the "Printer Icon" on your toolbox and then select "OK" when the dialogue box appears. A copy of your spreadsheet will be printed by the designated printer. Refer to Illustration II:5 for an example of what a printed spreadsheet of a data file looks like.

Congratulations! After you have actually done each of the above steps in this chapter, you will have created your first data file. Well maybe the congrats are premature. You have to actually do the first Lab activity at the end of this chapter before you will have had the opportunity to have successfully created your first data file. But we're off and running. Time to try it!

Illustration II:4

Creating an SPSS Data File

1. Getting Into SPSS
   Select SPSS Icon
   Spreadsheet format appears

2. Opening a New File
   Select File
   Select New
   Select Data

3. Naming Variables
   Click Mouse Twice
   Type Variable Name (limit to 10 characters)
   Select Type (select numeric)
   Select Labels
         Type in Variable Name Meaning, e.g., Sex means Gender
         Type in Value, e.g., "1"
         Type in Label, e.g., "female"
         Select Add after doing above two steps & repeat these 2 steps until
              all answer values and labels are entered
   Select Continue
   Select OK

4. Entering Data
   Click Mouse once for box desiring to enter data into
   Type in value, e.g., "1" (for male) or "2" (for female)
   Click Mouse once or hit enter key
   Click next box, etc. until done entering data for current session

5. Saving Data File
   Select File
   Select Save Data
   Select proper disk drive (e.g., a:\ )
   Type in name of file, e.g., Crime.sav
   Hit enter or click OK

6. Re-entering Existing Data File to Add More Data Select File
   Select Open
   Select Data
   Select name of file (make sure to select proper disk)
   Select OK (spread sheet format with data should appear)

7. Re-Saving Existing Data File to Save Added Data
   Select Open
   Select Save
   Select proper disk
   Select OK

8. Obtain Printed Copy of Spreadsheet
   Select Printer Icon on Toolbox
   Select OK

Illustration II:5   Example of Spreadsheet

	sex	age	status	freq	amount
1	female	18.00	freshman	1 or 2 per s	2-3 servings
2	female	19.00	sophomore	sev per mo	2-3 servings
3	female	20.00	junior	weekly	2-3 servings
4	female	21.00	senior	sev per wee	2-3 servings
5	male	18.00	freshman	1 or 2 per s	2-3 servings
6	male	19.00	sophomore	weekly	2-3 servings
7	male	20.00	junior	sev per wee	4-6 servings
8	male	21.00	senior	sev per wee	4-6 servings
9	female	18.00	freshman	never	none
10	female	20.00	junior	weekly	7-10 servin
11	male	19.00	sophomore	weekly	7-10 servin
12	female	18.00	freshman	1 or 2 per s	2-3 servings
13	female	19.00	sophomore	sev per mo	2-3 servings
14	female	20.00	junior	weekly	2-3 servings
15	female	21.00	senior	sev per wee	2-3 servings
16	male	18.00	freshman	1 or 2 per s	2-3 servings

APPLICATION QUESTIONS

1. What is the relationship between a data gathering tool, such as a questionnaire, and a codebook? How is a codebook useful?

2. When creating a data file in an SPSS spreadsheet do you need to label answer values for nominal, ordinal, grouped *and* ungrouped interval level variables? Explain.

3. Show yourself the SPSS tutorial for "Overview." Describe the various ways in which you could obtain a printed hard copy of a spreadsheet, output, or chart.

4. When re-accessing a saved spreadsheet, when would you select the "a:\" drive versus the server ("s:\")?

LAB SESSIONS

Session II:1

Create (and save) a data file using the "Student Alcohol Survey" Codebook used in this Chapter. Save your data file on your disk (drive A:\) and name it "A:\StuAlco.Sav". Use the following data for this lab. Obtain a printed copy of your completed spreadsheet and proof your data entry. E-mail your instructor to let him or her know of your success and any possible problems.

```
1 18 1 2 3
1 19 2 4 3
1 20 3 5 3
1 21 4 6 3
2 18 1 2 3
2 19 2 5 3
2 20 3 6 4
2 21 4 6 4
1 18 1 1 1
1 20 3 5 5
2 19 2 5 5
1 18 1 2 3
1 19 2 4 3
1 20 3 5 3
1 21 4 6 3
2 18 1 2 3
2 19 2 5 3
2 20 3 6 4
2 21 4 6 4
1 18 1 1 1
1 20 3 5 5
2 19 2 5 5
```

Session II:2

Create a codebook for the following questionnaire. Then create a data file for the data that is also included with this lab. Save it as "A:\Homework.Sav" and obtain a printed copy of the spreadsheet. Turn in a copy of your codebook and a copy of your spreadsheet.

STUDENT HOMEWORK QUESTIONNAIRE

Respondent Directions: Please circle the most correct answer or fill in the blank for each of the below. Thank you for your help in this study.

[1.] Which gender are you?
    a. female
    b. male

[2.] What is your current age (in years)? ____

[3.] What is your current educational status?
    a. high school student
    b. college/university student (undergraduate)
    c. graduate student

[4.] What is your current grade point average (GPA)?
    a. under 2.0
    b. 2.0 - 2.49
    c. 2.5 - 2.99
    d. 3.0 - 3.49
    e. 3.5 - 4.00

[5.] How many hours do you, on average, study per day during each semester? __

[6.] What is your major?
    a. Education
    b. Social Science
    c. Natural/Physical Science
    d. Business
    e. Math

Homework.sav Data

```
1 18 2 1 1 3
1 20 2 4 4 2
1 19 2 3 3 1
1 22 2 2 2 1
1 19 2 1 1 1
1 20 2 3 4 3
1 20 2 3 3 2
2 18 2 1 1 3
2 18 2 3 4 2
2 19 2 3 4 3
2 19 2 4 4 3
2 20 2 3 3 2
2 21 2 4 6 1
2 18 2 3 4 2
2 19 2 3 4 3
2 19 2 4 4 3
2 20 2 3 3 2
2 19 2 3 4 3
2 19 2 4 4 3
2 20 2 3 3 2
2 21 2 4 6 1
2 18 2 3 4 2
2 19 2 3 4 3
2 19 2 4 4 3
1 20 2 4 4 2
1 19 2 3 3 1
1 22 2 2 2 1
1 19 2 1 1 1
1 20 2 3 4 3
1 20 2 3 3 2
2 18 2 1 1 3
2 18 2 3 4 2
2 19 2 3 4 3
2 19 2 4 4 3
2 20 2 3 3 2
2 21 2 4 6 1
2 18 2 3 4 2
2 19 2 3 4 3
2 19 2 4 4 3
2 20 2 3 3 2
2 19 2 3 4 3
2 19 2 4 4 3
2 20 2 3 3 2
2 21 2 4 6 1
2 18 2 3 4 2
```

Session II:3

Access the "Boot.Sav" data file which is located on the server. Use the codebook (see Appendix) to help you digest what data is included in this study. Obtain a printed copy of the spreadsheet. E-mail your instructor a brief description outlining what this study is about, the types of variables available for doing data analysis, and suggest at least one hypothesis that one might test with this data.

Session II:4

Access the "Alco.Sav" data file which is located on the server. Use the codebook (see Appendix) to help you digest what data is included in this study. Obtain a printed copy of the spreadsheet. E-mail your instructor a brief description outlining what this study is about, the types of variables available for doing data analysis, and suggest at least one hypothesis that one might test with this data.

Session II:5

Examine the list of other data files found on the server. E-mail your instructor a brief description of the types of data available for use in this course.

CHAPTER 3

TAKING A FIRST LOOK AT YOUR DATA

After creating a codebook for your questionnaire and an SPSS data file, you were ready to gather your data and enter it into your data file. Now you are ready to take your first look at the data you gathered. You are ready to tabulate how the respondents answered your questions and to determine if there are any relationships of a "cause and effect" nature which might help to answer your original research question. In order to begin preliminary data analysis, you will need to know how to use four SPSS techniques. You will need to know how to obtain and interpret *frequency distributions*, how to *recode* variables, how to obtain and interpret *crosstabulations*, and how to use the *select if* option.

Distribution of Respondents

Frequencies. The first step is to examine the frequency distributions, i.e., tabulations, for the demographic variables and the substantive variables in our study. We examine the frequency distributions for all our demographic variables first in order to determine what our sample looks like. Are they primarily middle aged caucasian men? If that is the population we are interested in studying then it is good that we ended up with such a sample. The demographic variables help us to determine if our sample is representative of the population we seek to study. Men and women of all ages and races must be present in our sample in the correct proportions. If our sample is not representative, then we better do something about that problem. Hence, we start with the frequency distributions of the demographic variables, e.g., gender, age, race, socio-economic status, education, religion.

After considering the demographics, we turn to an examination of the frequency distributions of the substantive variables. The substantive variables are those which will help us assess our research question. For example, if we are interested in voter opinions concerning an upcoming election, we would want to know which candidate is currently most preferred by the voters, how likely they are to actually vote on election day, and so forth. If we were interested in delinquent behavior, we may have asked the respondent how many times they have been arrested as well as how many times their parents, siblings and friends have been arrested. Why? Perhaps we are testing the viability of differential association theory. The frequency distributions give us a picture of the voting behavior, in the first example, or the delinquent behavior in the latter illustration.

What does a frequency distribution look like? Please refer to Illustration III:1 to see an example of frequency distributions and the proper format for presenting this information in a report. Illustration III:1 includes a frequency distribution for a nominal variable, an ordinal variable, a grouped interval level variable, and an ungrouped interval level variable. Try to interpret the frequency distribution for each.

Illustration III:1   Example for Demographic Variables

Sex	f	%
1. Female	82	53%
2. Male	72	47%
	154	100%

Education		
1. Drop Out	14	9%
2. High School	40	26%
3. Some College	60	39%
4. College Grad	40	26%
	154	100%

Income
1. Less than $30,000	54	34%
2. $30,001 - $60,000	72	46%
3. $60,001 - $90,000	23	17%
4. $90,001 +	5	3%
	154	100%

Age
25	5	3%
26	6	4%
29	24	16%
33	12	8%
35	5	3%
39	13	8%
42	34	22%
48	18	12%
55	19	12%
62	10	6%
67	6	4%
77	1	1%
79	1	1%
	154	100%

Writing Format for Reporting. Sociologists follow a particular technical writing style when reporting the frequency distributions for both the demographic and substantive variables. This writing style includes the use of sub-titles, delineation (expressed in words not numbers) of the observations for the answer categories for each variable, and the parenthetic inclusion of the actual observed percentages. The following serves as an example.

Demographic Distributions
   Gender & Age Composition. The current sample consisted of an almost equal number of females (53%, please see Table 1) and males (47%), with females slightly outnumbering males. The respondents ranged in age from 25 to 79 years of age. The sample was primarily middle-aged with approximately two-thirds of the respondents (65%) ranging between ages 33 and 55.
   Education. The sample consisted of a rather educated group of people. A majority (55%) of the respondents had either attended college or completed a college education. Approximately one-third of the sample were high school drop outs (9%) or high school graduates (26%).
   Income. The average respondent earned approximately $45,000 last year as almost half (46%) had earned between $30,000 - $60,000. A third (34%) earned less than $30,000. The remaining respondents (20%) earned more than $60,000 last year.
   The typical respondent was found to be a middle-aged female who had a college education and earned approximately $45,000 last year. This individual could be considered middle-class.

Substantive Variables

Drinking Behavior. A majority (58%, please see Table 2) of the respondents reportedly place themselves in a drinking situation no more than once a week. Approximately a third (36%) do so twice a week, while a few (6%) go out to parties at least three times a week. While in attendance, the average respondent consumes no more than one alcoholic beverage per drinking episode (60%). Most of the remaining respondents (38%) reportedly consume two or three such beverages, while only a few (2%) indulge in more serious consumptive patterns, i.e., more than four drinks per episode.

Notice that the frequency distributions for the demographic variables become "Table 1" and those of the substantive variables become "Table 2." This tradition is followed even if there are multiple variables per table. The goal in reporting on the tabulated demographics and behaviors germane to the study is to paint a picture with words. The writing should take the reader by the hand and lead him or her through the frequency distributions in order to provide a mental picture of the demographic makeup and behavioral responses reported to the researcher.

Obtaining Frequency Distributions From SPSS. After obtaining the desired data file in the spreadsheet, it is very easy to obtain desired frequency distributions. Simply select "Statistics," then "Summarize," and finally "Frequencies." When the dialogue box appears, designate the variables for which you desire frequency distributions by using the mouse to highlight and move them from the left box to the right box. Select "OK" and the frequencies will appear in the output window.

Use the directional arrows to help you view the entire contents of the output window. For each variable, you will find the variable name, values, frequency of each value, percentage for each value, valid percentage, and cumulative percentage as well as the incidence of missing data. Refer to Illustration III:2 for an summarized reference list of these steps.

Printing. To obtain a print out of any output window you follow the same procedure as you did for printing a spreadsheet. While the output window is on the monitor, use the mouse to select the printer icon in the tool box. After confirming the appropriate printer has been selected (select "OK"), the frequencies, in this case, will be printed. Illustration III:3 is an example of the output you would view in the output window and obtain through using the printing function.

Saving. If you would like to save this output on your disk for future reference, select "File," then select "Save As," designate disk "a:" as the destination, and name your output file. An example of a name for your output file might be "Study.Lst" (if you were working with a data file that you named "Study.Sav") to save obtained frequencies. The "Study.Lst" designation will tell the computer that your output is for data you are naming as "Study" and the suffix "Lst" is the required designation for an output window's contents.

Graphics. You could also obtain a graphic portrayal of your frequency distributions by selecting any of the graphic options available such as a bar graph or a pie chart. Simply select "chart" and then select the desired graphic form. Designate the desired variable in the dialogue box and after indicating "OK," you will obtain the selected graphic in another output window. If you would like a printed copy, follow the previously indicated procedure for obtaining a print out. If you would like to save this chart, follow the previously indicated procedure for saving a file. One difference: the suffix must read ".Cht" because this is the "Chart" designation required by SPSS, e.g., "Study.Cht" would be appropriate for the current example. Illustration III:4 is an example of what the chart would look like in the output window and if you requested a printed copy.

Illustration III:2   Frequency Distributions

Getting the Frequencies
Get Spreadsheet of Data File Up on Screen
Select Statistics
Select Summarize
Select Frequencies
Select each variable and move over to right box
Select desired statistics & chart (if desired)
OK

Viewing the Frequencies
When Output Appears on screen:
Use up/down arrows to scroll thru output window
Obtain print out of hard copy of frequency tables if desired
Save frequency tables into a new saving file if desired

Reading Tables
Note variable name top left of table
note value label and values (yes - 1; no - 2)
note frequency = number of respondents answering Yes or No
note percent = percent of total answering Yes or No (with missing included)
valid percent = percent of total answering Yes or No (missing excluded)
cum percent = cumulative percentage (Yes; Yes + No; etc.)
note # of valid cases & # of missing cases reported

Illustration III:3   Frequency Distribution Output

AGE1   recoded age

Value Label	Value	Frequency	Percent	Valid Percent	Cum Percent
underage	1.00	18	81.8	81.8	81.8
legal age	2.00	4	18.2	18.2	100.0
	Total	22	100.0	100.0	

Valid cases   22   Missing cases   0

- -

AMOUNT1   recoded amount

Value Label	Value	Frequency	Percent	Valid Percent	Cum Percent
3 drinks or less	1.00	14	63.6	63.6	63.6
4 drinks or more	2.00	8	36.4	36.4	100.0
	Total	22	100.0	100.0	

Valid cases   22   Missing cases   0

- -

FREQ1   recoded freq

Value Label	Value	Frequency	Percent	Valid Percent	Cum Percent
monthly or less	1.00	8	36.4	36.4	36.4
weekly or more	2.00	14	63.6	63.6	100.0
	Total	22	100.0	100.0	

Valid cases   22   Missing cases   0

Illustration III:4   Chart Print Out

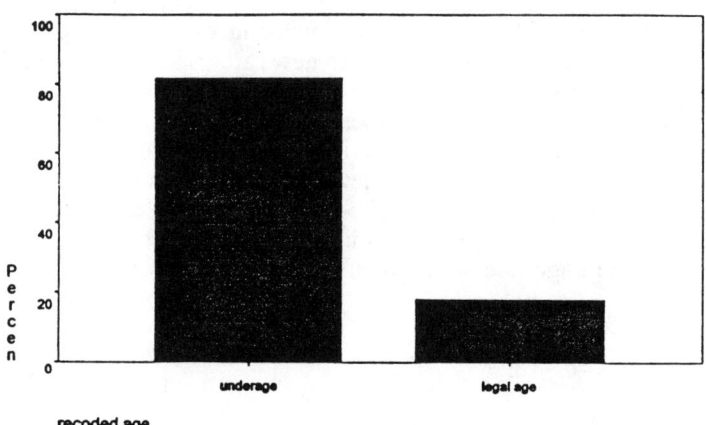

recoded age

Recoding Variables

Do you remember the frequency distribution for age included in Illustration III:1? Take another look. Doesn't this presentation look odd to you? What if the age distribution included almost every possible integer between ages 1 and 100? Wouldn't this be a rather long and awkward table? There are circumstances under which the researcher recodes the original data into new categories. The current age data is one good example of just such a circumstance. Recoding can be done for any type of variable, nominal, ordinal, grouped or ungrouped interval level variables. It is almost always required when working with an ungrouped interval level variable. Such variables are usually recoded pursuant to their presentation in a frequency distribution. For example, presentation would be much better if we recode the noted age data as follows:

Age	f	%
18 - 30	35	23%
31 - 55	101	65%
56 +	18	12%
	154	100%

Recoding "Rules." So how do you decide where the boundaries will be between newly grouped, i.e., recoded, categories? If, for example, you want to recode age from an ungrouped interval level variable into two categories that make sense for a study of alcohol consumption patterns, how should you proceed with recoding? The first rule of thumb is to ask yourself if there is some sociological *logic* involved in what the desired outcome should look like. In a study on alcohol consumption patterns you might want to logically look at the drinking behavior of those who are of legal age versus those who are underage. If that is the case, you want to recode age into two groups: those 20 years of age and under versus those who are 21 and older. Logic was our guide here.

The other rule of thumb, if there is no sociological logic apparent, is to use the mean or median. For example, you may want to compute the average number of parties a student has attended this academic year and then divide the students into two groups. The first group would consist of those who have attended less than the average number of parties while the second group would consist of those who attended at least the average number. To summarize, our first rule is to let logic guide our recoding, if none prevails then we use the mean or median. [An alternate version of the second rule is to use percentiles if we want more than one category, e.g., 25th percentile, 50th percentile, 75th percentile, and 100th percentile--or some other numerical variation such as thirds.]

Using SPSS to Recode & Relabel Variables. After obtaining the desired data file spreadsheet, select "Transform," then select "Recode," then you must make a decision. Do you want to recode the variable and save these recodes in the same column as the old variable coding (thus erasing the original data) or do you want to create a new variable which contains these recoded values? I would recommend that, as a rule, you do not erase original data. Create a new column. For example, keep your original "Age" data in its original form and column. Add a new variable to your data spreadsheet named "Age1" which contains the same age information, but in recoded form. How? After selecting "Recode," then select "Different Variable." Indicate the desired new name and from the dialogue box indicate the desired variable to be recoded and indicate the ranges and values of the new codes. The computer will automatically create the new variable "Age1" and do the recoding. [You may wish to refer to the SPSS text and the Tutorial for more details. Also speak with your instructor.] The process for selecting variables and labeling the new recoded values is the same as when you are originally entering variables into a spreadsheet--please refer to Chapter 2. The primary difference you will find is in the recoding process. Here you must specify the ranges and the recoded values for these ranges. See Illustration III:5 for a summarized list of the recoding steps.

Saving Recodes. Since you have added new data to your data file, you will want to save these changes for possible future use. From the spreadsheet, select "File," then select "Save," and "OK" in order to save your recoded variable(s). Whenever you want to work with this data again, you will not have to go through the recoding process. If you have only recoded one variable, it is not an onerous task to redo the recoding. If, on the other hand, you have recoded several variables, saving these changes will save allot of time in the future. See Illustration III:6 for an example of a spreadsheet which contains the original data on education, "educ," and the recoded version, "neweduc."

Illustration III:5   Recoding Variables

Recoding
Get Spreadsheet of Data File Up on Screen
Select Transform
Select Recode
Choose either Into Same Variable OR Into Different Variable
Select Variable you desire to recode & move to right box
[If Creating New Variable for Recoded Variable Name Now]
Select Old/New
Type in Range of Values changing (recoding), e.g., you want to combine
           drop outs and high school grads and keep college grads
           separate (3 educ groups become 2):
           1 thru 2 = 2 and 3 = 3. So, you type in range 1 through 2, then
Select & Type new value, make high school drop outs and grads both a 2
Select Add
Type next range, in this example you select Old Value to stay same, type 3 and
Select & Type new value as 3 also
Select Add
Continue Above Recoding process on any other variables you desire to recode
OK (when done recoding)

Now you are ready to run freqs and/or crosstabs on variable(s) you recoded

Illustration III:6 Spreadsheet with Recoded Variables

	sex	age	status	freq	amount	age1	freq1	amount1
1	female	18.00	freshman	1 or 2 per s	2-3 servings	underage	monthly or l	3 drinks or l
2	female	19.00	sophomore	sev per mo	2-3 servings	underage	monthly or l	3 drinks or l
3	female	20.00	junior	weekly	2-3 servings	underage	weekly or m	3 drinks or l
4	female	21.00	senior	sev per wee	2-3 servings	legal age	weekly or m	3 drinks or l
5	male	18.00	freshman	1 or 2 per s	2-3 servings	underage	monthly or l	3 drinks or l
6	male	19.00	sophomore	weekly	2-3 servings	underage	weekly or m	3 drinks or l
7	male	20.00	junior	sev per wee	4-6 servings	underage	weekly or m	4 drinks or
8	male	21.00	senior	sev per wee	4-6 servings	legal age	weekly or m	4 drinks or
9	female	18.00	freshman	never	none	underage	monthly or l	3 drinks or l
10	female	20.00	junior	weekly	7-10 servin	underage	weekly or m	4 drinks or
11	male	19.00	sophomore	weekly	7-10 servin	underage	weekly or m	4 drinks or
12	female	18.00	freshman	1 or 2 per s	2-3 servings	underage	monthly or l	3 drinks or l
13	female	19.00	sophomore	sev per mo	2-3 servings	underage	monthly or l	3 drinks or l
14	female	20.00	junior	weekly	2-3 servings	underage	weekly or m	3 drinks or l
15	female	21.00	senior	sev per wee	2-3 servings	legal age	weekly or m	3 drinks or l
16	male	18.00	freshman	1 or 2 per s	2-3 servings	underage	monthly or l	3 drinks or l

Comparing Two Variables for a Possible Relationship

When a researcher begins to analyze her data, she begins by looking at the frequency distributions so that she can become familiar with the composition of the sample (demographic variables) and with the general behavior patterns of the respondents (substantive variables). After examining these initial tabulations, the researcher then takes the second step in data analysis which is to begin looking for possible relationships which may help to answer the research question. She will want to determine if the dependent variable(s) is influenced by any of the possible independent variables, which may be found among the demographic or substantive variables.

The level of measurement will dictate what statistical approach the researcher will take in assessing for possible relationships--as will be addressed in Chapter 5. For now, let's note that when the variables we seek to examine for a possible relationship are nominal variables, ordinal variables (with two or three answer categories, other wise they should be recoded into fewer such categories), or interval level variables which have been recoded so they can be treated like nominal or ordinal variables (recoded into two or three categories), then a common technique to employ is the cross-tabulation of a dependent variable with a possible independent variable. Looking at one pair of such variables at a time can facilitate a process of elimination when trying to identify possible "causes" for our behavior. [Statistical procedures for determining statistically significant relationships will be discussed in Chapter 5.]

For example, if we return to our earlier study on student drinking behavior, i.e, the "Student Alcohol Survey," we find three possible independent variables (Sex, Age, Status--which happen to all be demographic variables in this study) and two dependent variables which measure drinking behavior (Freq and Amount). Let's consider the following research question, "Under what circumstances are university students likely to consume large amounts of alcohol?" The data available in the current study would enable us to examine for the possible influence of gender, age, and class status on drinking behavior patterns. Perhaps we suspect that as college students become socialized into the student subculture, their consumption of alcoholic beverages increases both in terms of incidence and amount consumed per episode. The respondent was also asked to identify his or her gender and age. These additional two variables provide us with the opportunity to assess the role played by gender (Do males drink more than women--perhaps as a result of gender role socialization?) and age (perhaps older students drink more often and consume more because they have greater or easier access to alcohol). Let's look at the following table for an example.

		Status	
		Underclass	Upperclass
Freq			
	0-1 Per Week	60%	20%
	2 + Per Week	40%	80%
		100%	100%
N = 100		(56)	(44)

Notice that in the above example the independent variable is listed in the columns and the dependent variable is found in the rows. Also note that the percentages are computed *down the columns* which enables the researcher to determine if "Status" plays a role in the drinking frequency among the surveyed students. What do you think? Indeed, more than half (60%) of the underclassmen in this sample said that they infrequently consume alcoholic beverages while four-fifths (80%) of the upperclassmen indicate they frequently consume such beverages. The observed pattern suggests, at least tentatively, that the answer to our research question is: Yes, a socialization process is apparent. As new students become increasingly socialized into a student subculture, which includes a drinking norm, i.e., a norm which directs students to consume alcoholic beverages, they tend to drink more frequently. Of course, further research is necessary to control for the possible effects of gender, age, and other variables not included in the present study such as fraternity/sorority membership and grade point average. *[Notice the format of the language I just used to describe what I see in this table. Also note how I include the exact percentages in parentheses while I talk about the ratio of students using words. This paragraph should serve as an example of how you should report the findings of such tables.]*

Suppose, on the other hand, that you observed the following table rather than the one above:

		Status	
		Underclass	Upperclass
Freq			
	0-1 Per Week	60%	55%
	2 + Per Week	40%	45%
		100%	100%
N = 100		(56)	(44)

What would you tentatively conclude? A majority of both underclassmen (60%) and upperclassmen (55%) reportedly consume alcoholic beverages no more than once a week. There appears to be no real difference in drinking behavior regardless of class status. We could tentatively conclude that the previously hypothesized socialization process does *not* occur.

Report Writing Format & Table Presentation. Let's look at a formal example of how the researcher would write a description of what she is observing in a crosstabulation table. Let's use the previous example to illustrate this process. Once again, the writer should take the reader by the hand and walk him or her down the table painting a mental picture with *words*. Percentages are included only parenthetically. The paragraph in the report discussing a possible relationship between class status and drinking frequency might look something like:

WHAT VARIABLES INFLUENCE DRINKING BEHAVIOR?
Drinking Frequency Not Influenced by Class Status. It appears that the frequency with which one consumes alcohol does not vary by class status among college students. Both a majority of underclassmen (60%, please see Table 3) and a majority of upperclassmen (55%) drank no more than once a week. We find that upperclassmen are no more likely to be frequent party-goers than their underclass neighbors. Apparently the belief that a student subculture socializes students to become so-called party animals is incorrect.

Let's also look at an example of how the first version of these findings would be reported.

WHAT VARIABLES INFLUENCE DRINKING BEHAVIOR?
Upperclassmen More Likely to be Drinkers. It appears that a student subculture does indeed socialize students into a drinking culture. In the present study, a majority of underclassmen (60%) were found to consume alcohol no more than once a week while the more than three out of four upperclassmen (80%) reportedly consume alcohol at least twice a week. Students, administrators, parents, and taxpayers may want to consider the implications of this pattern in light of the dangers of alcohol abuse and alcoholism in contemporary American society.

Using SPSS to Obtain Crosstabulations. Working from the spreadsheet of the desired data file, select "Statistics," then "Summarize," and finally "Crosstabs." The dialogue box appears on your monitor. After determining which two variables you want to examine, move the dependent variable into the box for the row and the independent variable into the box for the column. You must be sure to put the dependent in the row and independent in the column or the computations will be incorrect. Next, select "Cells" and then

"Columns" so that the percentages will be computed down the columns. Select "OK" and the crosstabulations will appear in the output window. You may obtain a printed copy of the output and save the output by followed the same procedures used for frequency distributions. Illustration III:7 summarizes these steps.

Illustration III:7   Crosstabulations

Looking for Possible Association Between Two Variables:
Independent & Dependent Variables

Getting the Crosstabs
Get the Spreadsheet of the Data File Up on Screen
Select Statistics
Select Summarize
Select Crosstabs
Determine which two variables you want to look at for a possible association
Determine which variable is the Dependent Variable
Move the Dependent Variable into the right box (rows)
Determine which variable is the Independent Variable
Move the Independent Variable into the right box (columns)
Select Desired Statistic, if any (See NOTE below)
Select Cells Box & Select Columns
OK

Viewing the Crosstabs
When Output Appears on Screen:
        Use up/down arrows to scroll thru output window
        Obtain print out of hard copy of crosstabs table(s) if desired
Save Crosstabs table(s) in new file if desired

Reading Tables
Note Variables listed (I at top of table, D on left side)
Note value labels & numbers listed for each (top of each column and side
        of each row)
Read percentages DOWN the COLUMNS, they should sum to 100%, e.g., 75%
        of those having alcoholic parents are alcoholic while 25% are not;
        conversely (2nd column) 80% of those not having an alcoholic parent
        are not alcoholic (pattern!!!)
Note number of respondents in each cell too

Illustration III:8　　　　Crosstabulation Output

```
AMOUNT1   recoded amount  by  SEX  gender

                        SEX              Page 1 of 1
              Count
              Col Pct  female   male
                                            Row
                        1.00|    2.00| Total
AMOUNT1
                1.00     10       4        14
   3 drinks or less     83.3    40.0      63.6

                2.00      2       6         8
   4 drinks or more     16.7    60.0      36.4

              Column     12      10        22
              Total     54.5    45.5     100.0

Number of Missing Observations:  0
```

```
FREQ1   recoded freq  by  SEX  gender

                        SEX              Page 1 of 1
              Count
              Col Pct  female   male
                                            Row
                        1.00|    2.00| Total
FREQ1
                1.00      6       2         8
   monthly or less      50.0    20.0      36.4

                2.00      6       8        14
   weekly or more       50.0    80.0      63.6

              Column     12      10        22
              Total     54.5    45.5     100.0

Number of Missing Observations:  0
```

Controlling for the Possible Influence of a Third Variable

There are those occasions when you want to look at only a sub-population within the sample on which you have gathered data. For example, let's say that you are interested in the drinking patterns of only the men in your sample. You could use SPSS to select only the male respondents and then look at their drinking behavior. After selecting only the males, you could then obtain frequency distributions for drinking frequency and drinking amount. In so doing, you would examining the drinking pattern of only the males--not the entire sample. You are controlling for a third variable, in this case gender, by selecting only the men and then obtaining a crosstabulation for status and drinking frequency (as well as drinking amount). By examining such a crosstabulation you would be seeking to determine if underclass males were more or less likely to frequently consume alcohol (or large amounts of alcohol). After examining the frequency distributions and/or crosstabulations for only the males, you can obtain the frequencies and crosstabulations for only the females. The "select if" option provides the researcher with the opportunity to determine if two independent variables are influencing the dependent variable.

Let's work with an example. If you refer back to the first illustration of a crosstabulation comparing the possible effect of "Status" on "Drinking Frequency," the majority (80%) of the upperclassmen were found to be frequent drinkers while the majority (60%) of the underclassmen not frequent drinkers. However, when we control for gender we find that both status and gender play a role--but not an equal one. Below we find that while most (90%) of the male upperclassmen frequently drink and the majority (70%) of the male underclassmen do not, there is no difference in female drinking behavior. It appears that socialization into the student subculture has a greater impact on men.

	Status	
Drink Frequency	Male Underclassmen	Male Upperclassmen
0-1 Per Week	70%	10%
2 + Per Week	30%	90%
	100%	100%

Drink Frequency	Female Underclassmen	Female Upperclassmen
0-1 Per Week	53%	52%
2 + Per Week	47%	48%
	100%	100%

You may want to become even more sophisticated. You may want to control for more than one variable at the same time. For example, you may want to select young middle class males, i.e., select only the respondents who are young, who are middle class, and who are male. Status could then be crosstabulated with drinking frequency. The simple "select if" option enables the researcher to become as sophisticated as she seeks to be in building models to explain behavior.

Report Writing Style. The writing style and table format is really the same regardless of whether or not one controls for a third variable. The only difference is that we have more columns of information to present and describe. Returning to the previous example, instead of reporting on what the drinking frequency of underclassmen versus the upperclassmen, we are reporting on the drinking frequency of upperclass men versus the underclass men in contrast to the upperclass women versus the underclass women.

Using SPSS to "Select If." After obtaining the spreadsheet for the desired data file, select "Data," then "Select Cases," and then select the variable you want to control for. Select the "If" box, move the control variable into the work box, and then use the pad (in the dialogue box) to delineate the parameters you choose for the control variable. When you are finished indicating the parameters, select "Continue" and "OK." At this point you are ready to obtain the desired frequency distributions or crosstabs. If you controlled for gender, e.g., males only, you are ready to compare "status" with "drinking frequency." After obtaining this crosstabulation you would select only females and complete the second crosstabulation (caution: after you have eliminated all respondents except for those you are controlling for, e.g., men, you must bring all the respondents back before controlling for the remaining respondents, e.g., women).

Logical Expressions and Operators. When working from the pad to delineate parameters for the control variable, you will have several logical expressions available for your use. These options include the following:

EQ or = Equal to	NE or < > Not equal to
LT or < Less than	LE or < = Less than or equal to
GT or > Greater than	GE or > = Greater than/equal to

If you want to combine several conditions as part of the selecting process, you have several logical operators available. For example, if you want to select the respondent who is male *and* who is of sophomore status, then there are a few logical operators you may find useful:

And or &	And
Or	Or
Not	Not

Illustration III:9 summarizes the steps necessary to use the "select if" option for control for an additional variable(s).

Illustration III:9   Control for a Third Variable

Using Select If

Get the Spreadsheet of the Data File Up on Screen
Select Data
Select "Select Cases"
Select the variable you want to control for (Select If work to be done on),
     e.g., you want to control for education and look at possible association between having an alcoholic parent and alcoholism: So first you need to look at lower educated respondents & do crosstabs; then look at only highly educated respondents & do crosstabs
Select the If box
Select the Variable to work on & move to box
Use pad to delineate parameters, e.g., NewEduc < = 2 (high school drop outs
     & grads)
Select Continue
OK

Now go to work obtaining output for crosstabs between I and D var of interest, e.g., Alco and AlcoP

Then, return to Select If process outlined above to Select If for highly educated respondents:
Select if for NewEduc again, in this example, but change parameters from NewEduc < = 2, make it NewEduc > = 3
Then work run crosstabs for Alco and AlcoP for the highly educated
Look at output to determine if controlling for education impacted upon nature of the relationship observed between having an alcoholic parent or not on one's own chances of becoming alcoholic

Illustration III:10   Example of Select If Output

FREQ1   recoded freq   by   STATUS1   status1

Count Col Pct	STATUS1 undercla ssman 1.00	uppercla ssman 2.00	Row Total
FREQ1			
1.00 monthly or less	6 100.0		6 50.0
2.00 weekly or more		6 100.0	6 50.0
Column Total	6 50.0	6 50.0	12 100.0

Page 1 of 1

FREQ1   recoded freq   by   STATUS1   status1

Count Col Pct	STATUS1 undercla ssman 1.00	uppercla ssman 2.00	Row Total
FREQ1			
1.00 monthly or less	2 33.3		2 20.0
2.00 weekly or more	4 66.7	4 100.0	8 80.0
Column Total	6 60.0	4 40.0	10 100.0

Page 1 of 1

AMOUNT1   recoded amount   by   STATUS1   status1

Count Col Pct	STATUS1 undercla ssman 1.00	uppercla ssman 2.00	Row Total
AMOUNT1			
1.00 3 drinks or less	4 66.7		4 40.0
2.00 4 drinks or more	2 33.3	4 100.0	6 60.0
Column Total	6 60.0	4 40.0	10 100.0

Page 1 of 1

AMOUNT1   recoded amount   by   STATUS1   status1

Count Col Pct	STATUS1 undercla ssman 1.00	uppercla ssman 2.00	Row Total
AMOUNT1			
1.00 3 drinks or less	6 100.0	4 66.7	10 83.3
2.00 4 drinks or more		2 33.3	2 16.7
Column Total	6 50.0	6 50.0	12 100.0

Page 1 of 1

APPLICATION QUESTIONS

1. Using the proper report writing format, describe the following frequency distributions.

Age		Sex	
18 - 25	27%	female	65%
26 - 35	19%	male	35%
36 - 59	34%		100%
60 +	20%		
	100%		

Drinking Frequency Per Sitting

0 drinks	23%
1 - 2 drinks	55%
3 - 5 drinks	12%
6 + drinks	10%
	100%

2. Explain what frequency distributions are used for.

3. Using the proper report writing format, interpret the following table.

	Average Grades of Respondent	
Drinker Type	A/B Student	C/D Student
Moderate	85%	25%
Heavy	15%	75%
	100%	100%

4. Turn to Illustration II:2. Logically recode each of the following:

Status	Frequency
Age	Amount

5. Turn to Lab II:2. Logically recode the following:

GPA	Major

6. Turning back to Lab II:2, how would you use "Select If" to control for major if you want to compare study time with GPA?

LAB SESSIONS

Session III:1

Using the Student Alcohol Survey data from Chapter 2 (a:\StuAlco.Sav), obtain frequency distributions for all demographic and substantive variables. Write a report which describes the sample and the drinking behaviors of the respondents. Use proper writing style and table format for reporting these findings.

Session III:2

Using the Student Homework Survey data from Chapter 2 (a:\HomeWork.Sav), obtain frequency distributions for all demographic and substantive variables. Write a report which describes the sample and the study habits of the respondents. Use proper writing style and table format for reporting these findings.

Session III:3

Using the Student Alcohol Survey data, obtain the necessary crosstabulations to enable you to determine if any of the demographic variables influence student drinking behavior. Write a report using proper writing style and table format for reporting these findings.

Session III:4

Using the Student Homework Survey data, answer the following research question: what factors do and do not seem to influence how well a student performs, i.e., GPA? Also, control for "major" to determine if the patterns you observed vary from one major to another. Write a report using proper writing style and table format for reporting these findings.

Session III:5

Examine the codebook for the study on college drinking behavior (s:\Alco.Sav). Is drinking behavior affected by age, class, sex, or residence. Does type of drink appear to affect the patterns observed for age, class, sex or residence?

Session III:6

In the study on the Juvenile Bootcamp for Rehabilitation (Boot.Sav), does recidivism (24 months after program completion) appear to be less likely if they:
a. finished the program?
b. became a leader in the program?
c. were a member of a gang?
d. were well educated?
e. had relatives and friends with an arrest history?
f. returned to the old neighborhood?

CHAPTER 4

DESCRIPTIVE STATISTICS

Data analysts must report their findings to the appropriate audience when they have finished a research project. As noted in Chapter 1, academic researchers often report their findings through paper presentations at professional meetings such as the annual meetings of the American Sociological Association, Applied Sociological Association, or the Eastern Sociological Society. Research findings are also reported in nationally released reports by research centers. For example, my major research interest is the behavioral response to disasters. Research findings in the field of the sociology of disaster are often published by research centers such as the Disaster Research Center of the University of Delaware and the Natural Hazards Center of the University of Colorado. Research findings are also distributed through publication in scholarly journals, such as the *American Sociological Review*. A later version of the article you examined after reading the first chapter of this book was published in the *International Journal of Disaster Management*.

While most of you will create, analyze or use data, and disseminate it to others during the course of the average work day in your future career, you will probably not present your findings at sociology conferences or in academic journals. You will, however, be expected to report what you find to your boss or your client. The principles and statistics are the same in either case. The writing style will differ according to the audience and the work environment. If you master one, it is easy to acclimate oneself to other variations. Academics tend to teach their students the academic version they use; their students will then be positioned to go forth and adjust their training to the expectations and norms of their individual work environment. The computer skills you have been developing and the basic statistical skills that you are about to gain are required in any work environment.

The term "statistics" is often intimidating to people, but it should not be. Much "statistical analysis" involves the utilization of simple mathematical concepts which most us use on a daily basis. You will find that with an open mind and proper attitude "statistics" will not be intimidating. They provide you with an array of useful tools to help you understand what your respondents are telling you about their attitudes and behavior. Identifying and understanding their attitudes and behavior is enjoyable for any student of social science. So, let's embark on the next phase our journey.

Descriptive Statistics. As a researcher or data analyst you are expected to *describe and explain* the social reality you encounter. You are expected to describe the sample from which you gathered data and the answers this sample of respondents gave you (in Chapter 5 you will learn the statistical procedures that will help you to further explain your findings). The statistics commonly used to help in the descriptive process include: proportions, percentages, means, medians, modes, range, interquartile range (IQR), and standard deviation. Chapter 4 shows you how each is calculated by the computer and how to use them in describing your sample and research findings.

Proportions & Percentages

Proportions. Actually we have already been using proportions in this text. In the last chapter, I described what proportion of females (versus males) never drink, versus those who report drinking either several times a month, weekly, or more often than that. We observed that fully half, or one out of every two females reported never drinking alcoholic beverages. This one out of two, or one half, is, of course, a proportion. A proportion is simply the number of individuals or groups falling within the category you are examining, divided by the total number in all categories.

Proportion $P = f/n$
                   f = frequency or number in a category
                   n = total number in all categories

Let's look at an example. Suppose we interviewed 100 respondents, 50 men and 50 women. Let's further suppose that 25 of the women never drink and the rest drink as follows: 20 drink several times a month and 5 drink at least once a week. We find that the men, on the other hand, state that their drinking pattern is as follows: 10 of them never drink, 20 drink several times a month and the remaining 20 say they drink at least once a week. Let's look at a table which compares, or tabulates, these raw numbers by sex and drinking frequency. And, then we will describe what the drinking pattern is by sex, using proportions.

Table 1   The Effect of Gender on Drinking Frequency

	Sex	
	Female	Male
Drinking Frequency		
Never	25	10
Month	20	20
Weekly	5	20
	50	50

In order to determine the proportion of respondents engaging in any behavior, we use the raw numbers (as opposed to the percentages). The above table reports the "findings" by using raw numbers of respondents rather than percentages. Let's examine the column of females: what proportion of females reportedly never drinks? Answer: 1/2 (25/50). What proportion drinks monthly? Answer: 2/5's (20/50). Proportions are useful in helping us verbally describe what the observed relationship is among variables of interest in a report.

Writing Style. The following serves as an example of how to describe what we observe using proportions. It demonstrates how

> One hundred students were interviewed to determine the extent to which their drinking behavior varies by gender. There were fifty men and fifty women. Half of the women reportedly never drink, two-fifths drank at least once a month, and the remaining tenth drank at least once a week. Men drank more often. . . .

proportions are useful in describing what patterns are suggested by the tabulated data. It is far better to use proportions than to use the exact absolute numbers (or percentages in most instances). When someone reads your report, they want to obtain an impression of the relationships you examined-- parenthetically include specific numbers and refer the reader to your table when appropriate to do so. The researcher's job is to effectively communicate her findings. You must do this, however, by learning and following the technical writing format used in sociology. Proportions are but one simple tool to facilitate this process.

In addition to modeling your writing with proportions after the illustration above, you should examine a number of research journal articles or reports published by any agency. Turn to the findings section and use these articles or reports as models for your own work. You will be surprised how quickly you adjust to this technical writing style with a little practice.

Percentages. Throughout this book we have also been using our second tool, percentages. I know you already know how to compute this "statistic" as well. A percentage is an alternative to the proportion. It is simply a proportion in decimal form. Compute the proportion (actually divide the numerator by the denominator so that you change the form of the numerical relationship from a fraction into a decimal number) and multiply the decimal by 100.

$$\text{Percentage} \qquad \% = (f/n)100$$

Let's look at the same example we did for proportions using computed percentages instead of the absolute numbers. We previously said we interviewed 100 respondents, 50 men and 50 women (50% each). Let's look at an updated version of the table to see how the absolute numbers translate into percentages.

Table 1	Effect of Gender on Drinking Frequency	
	Sex	
	Female	Male
Drinking Frequency		
Never	50%	20%
Month	40%	40%
Weekly	10%	40%
	100%	100%
	(50)	(50)

Writing Style. The writing style should look familiar. It is the same format used in earlier chapters. As a reminder let's look at an example of how to report findings when percentages are involved.

> One hundred students were interviewed to determine the extent to which their drinking behavior varies by gender. Half of the sample (50%) were female and half (50%) were male. Half (50%) of the women reported never drinking, two-fifths (40%) drink at least once a month, and the remaining tenth (10%) drink at least once a week. Only a fifth (20%) of the men reported that they never drink. Two-fifths (40%) of the men reported drinking at least once a week. This is four times the number of women. Obviously men drink more frequently then women.

You can see how both percentages and proportions are useful in describing the observed behavior patterns. It is far better to use proportions than it is to use exact absolute numbers. Percentages are, in most instances, used only parenthetically. Remember, when someone reads your report, they want to be able to understand what you are trying to communicate. Proportions communicate more clearly then percentages. The percentages are to be given within parentheses right after you refer to the relationship with proportions. The researcher's job is not complete until she effectively communicates her findings. Proportions, combined with percentages, are simple tools used to facilitate this process.

Measures of Central Tendency

There are certain statistical measures available to the researcher which help us demographically describe the sample or population and help describe the attitudes and behavior for which data was gathered. The measures of central tendency include the mean, median, and mode. Please note that these measures are only useful when working with interval level data, i.e., they are not suitable for nominal variables and are usually not used for ordinal variables either. The way in which these statistics are calculated varies if the data is in grouped versus ungrouped form. Ungrouped data is raw data in its original interval form. Grouped data is that which has been categorized. The methods for calculating the mean, median and mode will be discussed later in this chapter. First we look at those methods used for *ungrouped data.*

Ungrouped Data

Mean. As you know, the mean is the arithmetic average of all the values in a distribution. To obtain the mean, or average age of the respondents who returned the "Student Alcohol Survey" we would simply sum the ages of all the individuals in the study and divide that sum by the total number of individuals. Expressed as a formula, the mean is:

Mean $M = \text{Sum } X/N$

Sum X = the sum of all the values in the distribution
N = the number of values in the distribution

For example, nine respondents reported their ages as follows:

17, 22, 18, 18, 18, 19, 20, 21, 25

we determine their average age by adding all the values $(17+22+18+18+18+19+20+21+25)$ and dividing that sum by the number of values $(N=9)$. The mean age for this distribution is:

$M = 178/9 = 19.7$ or   20 years of age

Hence, in our example, the average age of those completing the "Student Alcohol Survey" is 20 years.

The mean is an appropriate measure to employ when the data you are trying to describe is interval level. It makes sense to talk about average age, average income, and average years of completed education. For ordinal data it is possible to determine the "mean category" or category in which the average case falls. If we were to use our "Freq" data, we could determine whether the average drinking frequency falls, for example, in the "once or twice a semester" category versus the "several times a week" category. But we are limited to using the mean for this type of application when the data is ordinal and it is often confusing for the data analyst. All too often the researcher obtains a mean of, say, "3" for the ordinal variable and, if she is not careful, she can misinterpret the three as being three drinks per week rather than category three. The mean is not an appropriate tool to use with nominal level variables. The "average gender or race" does not make sense.

Median. The median is the midpoint within a distribution of values which are ordered from highest to lowest value. The median of a distribution is the point at which 50% of the values are above it and 50% are below it. The median is a useful tool when describing interval (and sometimes ordinal) level data. It is inappropriate to calculate a median on nominal data, e.g., how could you have a median gender? The method for calculating the median varies with the number of cases in the distribution. If there is an odd number of values, then the median is simply the middle value when all the values are arranged in order from high to low.

Median (odd # of cases)   Median value = $(N + 1)/2$

where N = the number of cases or values in the distribution

For example, if nine respondents reported their ages as:

17, 22, 18, 18, 18, 19, 20, 21, 25

you would first re-arrange these ages in order from high to low (or vice versa):

17, 18, 18, 18, 19, 20, 21, 22, 25

The median value is calculated in this case to be:

Median value = $(N + 1)/2 = (9 + 1)/2 = 5$

The fifth case or value in the distribution is the median age for this sample. Note: 5 is not the median, the 5 means the 5th value in the distribution is the median value. Counting from left to right in the above line of ordered ages, the fifth value is "19." The median is nineteen years of age.

What happens when there is an even number of cases? The median is then the average of the middle two values in the distribution when the values have been arranged in order from high to low (or vice versa). Hence, the formula is:

Median (even # of cases)   [(N/2) + (N/2 + 1)] /2

For example, if the ordered values for an N = 10 are:

17, 18, 18, 18, 19, 20, 21, 22, 23, 25

then the values we used to calculate the median is determined in the following fashion:

[(N/2) + (N/2 + 1)]/2 =
[(10/2) + (10/2 + 1)]/2 =
[(5th case value) + (6th case value)]/2

Now we know that the median, when there are ten cases in a distribution, is the average of the 5th and 6th cases. When the cases are ordered from low to high (or vice versa) we simply count in from the left to obtain the actual scored value of the 5th and 6th cases. We then determine the average of these two values in order to obtain the median for the sample with an even number of cases.

[(Value of 5th case) + (Value of 6th case)]/2 =
(19 + 20)/2 = 19.5 or 20 years of age

Mode. The mode is the value that occurs most frequently in a distribution. The mode is often used with nominal and ordinal data to identify the response which has the greatest number of cases belonging to it. For example, the mode of the interval level variable "age" would be "18" because there are three respondents who were eighteen years of age and only one of each remaining age category. Hence the mode, that which occurs most often in the distribution, is eighteen.

17, 18, 18, 18, 19, 20, 21, 22, 23, 25

Let's now look at an example how to determine the mode for an ordinal variable such as "Freq:"

Frequency	Response
5 people	(1) Never Drink
2 people	(2) Drink Several Times a Month
3 people	(3) Drink Weekly
4 people	(4) Drink Several Times a Week

If we translate the above example into a numeral distribution of values representing how the 14 respondents in this example, we might find the distribution looking like:

1 2 3 4 4 3 1 3 4 2 4 1 1 1

The mode is the value which occurs most often in the distribution. In this example, that value is "1" because a one appears five times in the distribution, while two answer "2s," three answer "3s," and four answer "4s" appear. Hence, in the above example, the mode is answer "1" which means more people answered "Never Drink" than any other response.

Grouped Data

Mode. So far our examination of mean, median, and mode has assumed the data in the distribution is ungrouped. There are instances, however, when the questionnaire requested data from the respondent which is grouped into several answer categories. For example, instead of asking the respondent for her actual age, she may have been asked to indicate her age within a categorical range, such as:

　　__ 1. Under 18 years old
　　__ 2. 18 - 25　years old
　　__ 3. 26 - 55　years old
　　__ 4. Over 55　years old

Using the above example, we may find that our sample of 100 individuals breaks down into the following age categories: 22 respondents under 18 years of age, 38 between ages 18 and 25, 20 between ages 26 and 55, with the remaining 20 individuals over 55 years of age. When working with grouped data we treat the midpoint of the category or interval with the most cases in it as the mode. In the above example, there are more 18-25 year olds than any other age group. The midpoint would be 21.5 years of age (or rounded off, 22 years of age).

Median. Most researchers normally attempt to obtain data which is in ungrouped form. However, there are times when it is only available to the researcher in grouped (categorized) form. SPSS calculates the median and mean for grouped data by assuming that all values fall at the mid-points of each category. This results in slight computation errors, but we can accept these as being within what statisticians cite as an *acceptable margin of error*. There are occasions when only tables of grouped data are published, hence, you as a researcher should be capable of being able to hand compute the median and mean for grouped data. In these instances the grouped data formulas are needed in order to estimate measures of central tendency.

Equal-Sized Intervals. The category intervals should all be of equal width for grouped interval data in order to calculate the median and mean. For grouped data, we make the assumption that the values in each category are evenly distributed within the interval. This is why the intervals must be of equal size. Keep in mind that the median and mean for grouped data will, by necessity, be approximations, since we are not working with the exact values. In order to determine equal-sized intervals, follow this procedure:

> 1. determine the number of desired intervals;
> 2. determine the minimum width for each:
>   a. determine range (hi - low value)
>   b. add 1 to the range
>   c. divide the (range + 1) by # of intervals
>   [result: minimum width necessary,
>   (range + 1)/#intervals];
> 3. round to the appropriate whole number (if necessary).

For example, let's say we have data for which the highest age is 91, and the lowest age is 18. Furthermore, let's assume we decided that 4 intervals are necessary in our study [as a rule of thumb, the researcher attempts to designate a number of intervals which will enable approximately the same number of cases to fall in each and still have variation across the range of sampled respondents-- to the extent this is possible, for there may be little or no variation in some instances]. The range would be 73, or 91 - 18 = 73. Hence, an interval would be equal to (73 + 1)/4 or 18.5, which we round up to 19. This means that our intervals could be larger than 19, but must be no smaller than 19 in order to include all values in the distribution across the four categories.

It is not absolutely necessary for all intervals to be equal in width to calculate the mean. The median could be calculated regardless, but since we usually would calculate and use both, it makes sense to establish equal intervals at the beginning. Let's look at an example of how the median is computed when the data is grouped.

If we had data for the variable "age" (see example below), then even though the interval is 19, the real limit of the interval is 20.

Interval level data is, by definition, continuous data (which means that data is not always in whole numbers, but can continually appear across the continuum of decimal numbers, e.g., 1.1, 1.2, 1.5, etc.). Therefore, in order to anticipate the necessity for rounding decimal numbers to the whole numbers contained in the stated intervals, we must both subtract and add ".5" from each interval boundary so that the real limits reflect the continuous nature of such interval variables.

Age of Respondents in Sample Study

Age Interval	Real Limits	Freq	Cumulative Freq
18 - 37	17.5 - 37.5	262	262
38 - 57	37.5 - 57.5	190	452
58 - 77	57.5 - 77.5	135	587
78 - 97	77.5 - 97.5	17	604
Total		604	

In order to determine the Median by hand for grouped interval data we use the following formula:

$$Md = Lm + [(.5N - CFbm)/Fm] \, I$$

Lm	=	lower real limit of interval containing the Median value
N	=	total number of values in distribution
CFbm	=	cumulative frequency of interval below the interval containing the Median value
Fm	=	frequency of interval that contains Median value
I	=	real limit interval width

In order to determine the interval that contains the median value, we must divide N by 2 and then look down the cumulative frequency column until we find the interval that contains N/2. In the example above, this would be $604/2 = 302$. The first interval contains 262 cases, the second interval contains 190 cases. Looking at the cumulative frequency column we find that cases number 302 falls between 262 and 452, i.e., the 302nd case falls in the second interval. So the median case falls in the interval defined as 38-57 (real limits 37.5-57.5). Applying the formula to the example table, we find:

$$Md = 37.5 + [\{.5(604) - 262\}/190] \, 20 = 37.5 + 4.21 = 41.71$$

When SPSS calculates the median for grouped interval data it will simply use the midpoint of the interval that contains the median value. Instead of a median of 41.7, SPSS would give us a median of 47.5. However, it may sometimes be desireable for you to hand calculate the median when the tables are published in grouped form and you do not have access to the raw data. You can use the above formula to do so.

Mean. The Mean for grouped interval data is calculated using the following formula:

Mean	=	Sum F(Xm) / N
Sum F(Xm) =		sum of the frequencies in each interval multiplied by the midpoint of each interval

Applied to the sample above, we multiple the midpoint of each interval times the frequency of cases appearing in each interval and sum these calculations as follows:

Real Limits Midpoint		Freq		F (Xm)
27.5	x	262	=	7,205.0
47.5	x	190	=	9,025.0
67.5	x	135	=	9,112.5
87.5	x	17	=	1,487.5
		604		26,830.0

Mean	=	Sum F(Xm)/N	=	26,830/604	= 44.2

Keep in mind that the mean for grouped interval data is an estimate because we are assuming that the actual values are distributed evenly across the intervals, which is, of course, unlikely. But this is the best estimate possible when working with grouped data. If we had access to the actual raw data values, the actual mean would, in almost all instances, be slightly different. We accept the grouped data estimate as being within an acceptable margin of error. Do you see one of many reasons why we strive to obtain interval level data which is not grouped?

Measures of Dispersion

Measures of dispersion are statistical calculations which tell the researcher how widely the data is distributed across the range from the mean. These measures tell us if most of the respondents are very similar (narrow spread across the distribution) or if they are very diverse in the attitudes or behavior studied (broadly spread across the distribution). The most common measures of dispersion are the range, the interquartile range (IQR), and the standard deviation (Variance is another, but it is essentially used by Sociologists as a step pursuant to calculating the standard deviation, as you will see below). As with measures of central tendency, the computation of range, IQR, and sd varies if the interval data is grouped versus ungrouped. We will consider ungrouped data first.

Ungroupd Data

Range. The range is simply the difference between the highest and lowest values in a distribution. Consider, for example, the following ages:

$$17, 34, 25, 35, 42, 55, 18, 63, 33$$

The range for this distribution of ages would be computed as follows:

Range   =   63 (highest)   -   17 (lowest)   =   46

This statistic is easily affected by extremes, e.g., a very high or very low value could distort one's impression of the respondents. Most respondents may be between the ages of 25 and 55, but if you had one individual who was 92 years old the range would be: 92 - 17 = 75 which gives the impression that the ages of the respondents in the study are spread across a continuum beginning with 17 and ending with 92. So, while the Range is a useful piece of information, its use is limited. It is primarily used to describe interval level data, but can also be used with ordinal variables. It is not applicable to nominal data.

Interquartile Range (IQR). The Interquartile Range enables the researcher to avoid the limitations of the range's sensitivity to extreme values. It calculates the middle 50% of the values across the distribution, eliminating those extreme values which may appear at either end of the distribution. The IQR is, therefore, the difference between the third and the first quartile:

IQR   =   Q3   -   Q1

Consider age data for the following twelve respondents:

$$17, 34, 25, 35, 42, 55, 18, 63, 33, 92, 54, 20$$

In order to find the values for the third and first quartiles, we must first re-arrange the age values from low to high (or vice versa):

$$17, 18, 20, 25, 33, 34, 35, 42, 54, 55, 63, 92$$

Even Number of Cases. Quartiles are, by definition, quarters. We must find the value of the first and third quarters (or fourths) of the distribution. There are 12 cases (even number) in the current example. To find the values of the first quarter we must simply multiple twelve by 1/4 and then look for the first value that exceeds this number. To obtain the value of the third quarter we must multiply twelve by 3/4:

Q1	=	[(12)/4] + 1	=	4th Value
Q3	=	(12)3/4	=	9th Value

Which numbers are the first and third quartile values?

14, 18, 20, <u>25</u>, 33, 34, 35, 42, <u>54</u>, 55, 63, 92

The numbers are "25" and "54." Notice that there are three values to both the left and the right of the quartile values. The IQR is then computed by finding the difference between these two values.

IQR   =   54 - 25   =   29

How do we interpret "29?" By saying that the IQR = 29 we are saying that 50% of all the respondents were within 29 years of each other (in this study that is between 54 and 25 years of age).

Odd Number of Cases. If there are an odd number of cases in the distribution (odd number of respondents), then you will not obtain a whole number when you multiple N by 1/4 or by 3/4. What do you do? Well, you select the value of the closest number when rounding up or down (following the rules for rounding: 3.75 becomes 4 and 11.25 becomes 11). So, in this example, if Q1 = 3.75 you select the value of the 4th case. If Q3 = 11.25, you select the value of the 11th case 11.

Standard Deviation. Range and IQR are both rather crude measures of dispersion. A more sophisticated measure is the standard deviation of the distribution of scores around the distribution's mean. Variance is actually computed, the square root of the variance is the standard deviation. These measures are based upon the following mathematical properties:

1. The sum of the differences of each value in a distribution from the mean of the distribution is equal to zero.

2. The sum of the squared differences of each value in a distribution from the mean of the distribution yields the minimum value. Squared differences of each value from another other value in the distribution will result in a higher number than using the mean to calculate the differences.

These mathematical principles translate into the following formula for computing the standard deviation for a sample. One computes the square root for:

$$[\text{Sum} \ (X - \overline{X})^2] \ / \ (N - 1)$$

$\underline{X}$	=	each value
$\overline{X}$	=	sample mean squared
N	=	sample size (number of respondents)

In other words, find the difference between the value and the mean for each case, square these differences, sum these squared differences and divide this sum by (N-1). Take the square root of this number and you have computed the standard deviation.

An alternative formula, which is much easier to use for hand tabulations, and is the algebraic equivalent of the above formula, is computed as follows. Compute the square root of:

$$\{\text{Sum } X^2 \ - \ [(\text{Sum } X)^2 \ / \ N]\} \ / \ (N - 1)$$

In other words, (1) square each value and sum these squares. From this sum subtract the following: (2) sum the values and square this total and then divide it by the total number of cases in the study. After subtracting (2) from (1) above, then divide this number by N - 1. The result? The result is the computed standard deviation. Let's try our hand at calculating a standard deviation for the following sample of nine values:

87, 92, 47, 58, 87, 62, 73, 73, 61

First, we need to compute the appropriate "squares:"

$\underline{X}$	$\underline{X}^{2}$
87	7,569
92	8,464
47	2,209
58	3,364
87	7,569
62	3,844
73	5,329
73	5,329
61	3,721
640	47,398

Applying our alternative formula for easier hand tabulations, we obtain a standard deviation of 15.36.

$$s^{2} = \{47{,}398 - [(640)^{2} / 9]\} / (9 - 1)$$
$$= 235.86$$
$$s = 15.36 \text{ years if age}$$

Use and Interpretation. Okay, we've calculated a standard deviation. So what? How is it useful in describing the degree of dispersion around the mean in our data's distribution? Well, by definition (another mathematical property at work here), one standard deviation accounts for 33.13% of the cases either above or below the mean, i.e., if a respondent scores within one standard deviation, she is keeping company with 33.13% of the individuals in this sample. The way we usually use standard deviation is to determine the point at which 66.26% of the people fall plus or minus one standard deviation of the mean (+/- 33.13% from the mean). If, as in the above example, s = 15.36 years of age. Then we can say that 66.26% of those samples fall within +/- 1 standard deviations of the mean age (which is 71.11 for this sample). Or, 66.26% of the people fall between the ages of 56 and 86. We round off age since it makes little sense to describe a person as being 71.11 years of age or 15.36 years from 71.11. We compute in the following way:

$$71 - 15 = 56 \qquad \& \qquad 71 + 15 = 86$$

Approximately two-thirds (66.26%) of the people are between the ages of 56 and 86 (or within 1 SD of the mean age which is 71 years of age).

Two standard deviations accounts, by definition, for 47.73% of the individual cases. Or, +/- two standard deviations account for 95.56%

of the cases. When applied to the above sample:

$$71 - 30 = 41 \qquad \& \qquad 71 + 30 = 101$$

Most (approximately 95%) of the people are between the ages of
41 and 101. Obviously this sample is of an older sub-sample of
the entire U.S. population and not the entire U.S. population.

It is important to remember what plus or minus one standard
deviation and two standard deviations means in terms of these
percentages. The mathematical computations and principles behind
standard deviation and its relationship to properties of the normal
curve are beyond the scope of this course. I ask that you take as fact
that mathematics tells us that the computed value for the "s" enables
us to calculate the points between which approximately 67% and 95%
of the sample fall. Obviously if most of them fall within a few points
(numbers) on the continuum, then the dispersion is very narrow.
Conversely, if they fall between two points that a very distant, then
the dispersion is very broad. For example, we have test scores for
two sections of the same Sociology course which look like the
following:

Section 01:	Mean = 75	&	1 sd = 20
Section 02:	Mean = 82	&	1 sd = 5

Usage and Writing Style. Which class did better on the exam?
Well, on the one hand, someone must have earned an "A" on the test
in Section 01 because +/- one standard deviation results in 67% of
the class falling between a low grade of 55 (75-20) and a high grade
of 95 (75+20). On the other hand, Section 02 did better as a group
because 67% of them scored between a low grade of 77 (82-5) and
a high grade of 87 (82+5). Furthermore, the mean for Section 02
was higher (82 versus 75). Do you see how this measure of
dispersion can be a useful statistic to have to describe attitudes or
behavior? I hope so, if this is not the case, see your professor for
further explanation.

Grouped Data

As with measures of central tendency, the formula for computing
standard deviation varies when the data is grouped. When hand
tabulating one must establish equal intervals, determine the
midpoints, and control for variation in frequency in the intervals. We
will not further examine the process of calculating measures of
dispersion for grouped data, however. Your exposure to how this is

done for measures of central tendency is enough to gain your appreciation of what SPSS is doing for you to save you time.

Report Writing Style Using Descriptive Statistics

Let's review. In addition to percentages and proportions, we can use the mean, median and mode as well as the range, (rarely the interquartile range), and the standard deviation to describe our demographic and substantive variables. Of course, just because we have these tools available to us, does not suggest that we always use them. We do so when it makes sense. For example, we would normally use either the mean or the median, but not both. We would only use the median if it differs dramatically from the mean. Why? If the median differs greatly that is because there is one (or a few) respondent who is skewing the distribution. What do I mean? Well if Donald Trump joined our class and I asked each of you to complete a questionnaire which included a question asking your annual income I think Mr. Trump's income would be significantly greater than anyone else's, including your professor's. Therefore, the average income for our class might be $345,000! The median income should be used instead.

The following is an example of the appropriate reporting style when using descriptive statistics with demographic and substantive variables. "Age" is, of course, a demographic variable; "Number of Study Hours" is an example of a substantive variable.

Age. The average respondent was 23 years of age. The respondents ranged in age from 15 to 74. Since approximately two-thirds of the respondents fell between ages 21 and 25 (mean = 23, standard deviation = 2 years), the typical respondent was apparently a college student. Turning to Table 1, we see that few respondents were under 18 years of age (5%), while most were between 18 and 25 (87%), with the remainder being non-traditional students (8%).

Number of Study Hours. The respondents reported investing an average of five hours preparing for class each week, e.g., reading assignments, homework questions, computer lab work and lab reporting. Some variation was observed in study habits, however. Some students reported investing as little as one hour a week (3%, see Table 4). Most students (85%) reported studying four to six hours a week. The remainder studied as least seven hours (12%) with one reporting an average of twelve hours a week. Approximately two-thirds reportedly study between four and six hours a week (mean = 5, standard deviation = 1 hour) which suggests that their study habits are pretty similar.

Using SPSS to Obtain Desired Descriptive Statistics

You can obtain descriptive statistics, e.g., mean, standard deviation, range, on any interval level variables in a data file, by using an appropriate SPSS Command. There are actually several ways to go about doing it. (1) From the spreadsheet environment of the data file you are working with, select "Statistics," then "Summarize," then "Descriptives," finally select and move the desired variables and select the desired statistical options. Select "OK" and a descriptive table will appear in your output window. (2) Alternately, you could select "Statistics," then select "Frequencies," and as you select the variables you want frequency distributions for, you can also select the desired statistics. The descriptive statistics will then be printed along with the frequency distributions in your output window when you select "OK." Most of the time it makes more sense to do the second option for obtaining descriptives since you usually also want the frequencies anyway. Illustration IV:1 summarizes these steps. Illustrations IV:2 and IV:3 provide examples of the output obtained as a result of the two options available for obtaining descriptives.

Illustration IV:1   Descriptive Statistics

Getting Descriptives

Option 1:

Get Spreadsheet of Data File Up on Monitor
Select Statistics
Select Summarize
Select Descriptives
Select & Move Desired Variables
[Select Desired Options]
OK

Option 2:

Get Spreadsheet of Data File Up on Monitor
Select Statistics
Select Frequencies
Select & Move Desired Variables & Desired Statistics
OK

Viewing Descriptives

When Output Appears on Screen:
    Use up/down arrows to scroll thru output window
    Obtain Print out of hard copy if desired
    Save results in lst (list) file if desired

Reading Table

Note var name given in first left column
Note each mean is in second column
Note Standard Deviation is in third column (approx. 2/3's of sample fall
    within +\- 1 sd if mean
Note minimum and maximum values in sample
Note number of respondents
Note last column is var labels

Illustration IV:2   Descriptive Statistics - Option 1

Number of valid observations (listwise) =   22.00

Variable	Mean	Std Dev	Range	Minimum	Maximum	Valid N
AMOUNT	3.36	1.09	4.00	1.00	5.00	22
FREQ	4.27	1.75	5.00	1.00	6.00	22
AGE	19.36	1.09	3.00	18.00	21.00	22

Illustration IV:3 Descriptive Statistics - Option 2

AGE

Value Label	Value	Frequency	Percent	Valid Percent	Cum Percent
	18.00	6	27.3	27.3	27.3
	19.00	6	27.3	27.3	54.5
	20.00	6	27.3	27.3	81.8
	21.00	4	18.2	18.2	100.0
	Total	22	100.0	100.0	

Mean	19.364	Median	19.000	Mode	18.000
Std dev	1.093	Range	3.000	Minimum	18.000
Maximum	21.000				

* Multiple modes exist. The smallest value is shown.

Valid cases   22   Missing cases   0

APPLICATION QUESTIONS

1. If you gathered data on a sample of 100 students with 40 of them reporting that they never drink, 40 of them reporting that they sometimes drink, and 20 of them reporting that they frequently drink:

    (a) what proportion of this sample constitutes frequent, potentially problem, drinkers?
    (b) What proportion of the sample drinks occasionally?
    (c) What percentage of the sample drinks frequently?
    (d) What percentage never drinks?

2. Five respondents report drinking according to the following patterns:

    #1 drinks once a week
    #2 drinks three times a week
    #3 drinks once a week
    #4 drinks daily
    #5 drinks twice a week

    (a) What is the average incidence of drinking among this sample?
    (b) What is the median incidence?
    (c) What is the mode?

3. If a sixth drinker reported drinking everyday, what would be the median?

4. If you obtained the following data:

# Respondents	Drinking Frequency
20	0 - 3 times per week
40	4 - 6 times per week
40	7 - 10 times per week

    (a) What is the mean drinking frequency for this sample?
    (b) What is the median drinking frequency?
    (c) The mode?

5. (a) What is the range for the data in Question #2 above?
   (b) What is the range for the data in Question #3 above?

6. (a) What is the Interquartile Range for the data in question #2
       above?
   (b) What is the Interquartile Range for the data in question #3
       above?
   (c) What is the interquartile range for the following data?

       17, 34, 34, 26, 42, 55, 17, 64, 32, 93, 54, 20

7. What is the mean, median, mode, range, IQR, and standard
deviation for the data in Question #6 above?

8. Use your findings to Question #7 to describe this sample (assume
the data is for the Ages of the respondents).   Use proper
language/writing style as demonstrated in this chapter of the book.

LAB SESSIONS

Session IV:1

Obtain the descriptive statistics for each of the appropriate variables in StuAlco.Sav. E-mail the descriptives for each appropriate variable, e.g., age: mean = 34, median = 34, mode = 22, range = 15-89, sd = 5.

Session IV:2

Obtain the descriptive statistics for each of the appropriate variables in Homework.Sav. E-mail the descriptives for each appropriate variable.

Session IV:3

Obtain the descriptive statistics for each of the appropriate variables in Alco.Sav. Also obtain a frequency distribution for each of these variables and e-mail a paragraph (for each the appropriate variables) describing it--making sure to include the descriptives in proper report writing language.

Session IV:4

Obtain the descriptive statistics for each of the appropriate variables in Boot.Sav. Re-write your Boot.Sav demographic and substantive variable descriptives to include the proper use of descriptive statistics when appropriate. Turn in this new wordprocessed version of your Boot.Sav report.

CHAPTER 5

EXPLANATORY STATISTICS

In the last chapter we examined simple statistical tools often used by researchers to describe the sample and the patterns indicated by the respondent's answers. While much social research is conducted at a level which requires only the use of descriptive statistics, e.g., percentages, ranges, and standard deviations, there is also a great deal of research which requires the use of more sophisticated statistical tools to test hypotheses, to ascertain the extent to which variables may influence one another, or to determine the extent to which patterns change over time. In order to accomplish these additional tasks, we draw upon tools which are often referred to as explanatory statistics.

When a researcher reports her findings, the first two subsections of the Findings Section of the report usually contains a sample description and a summary of the substantive findings. Descriptive statistics are all that is needed to help describe interval level variables in these two sections. The third subsection of the Findings is devoted to explaining the nature of the relationships of interest. This analysis often calls for the use of appropriate explanatory statistics which help the researcher to answer the research question. The most frequently used explanatory, or inferential, statistics in social research, and, therefore, those which we will study, include: Chi-Square, t-test, linear correlation and regression, as well as multiple regression. Chi-Square is designed to test for a possible association between two nominal level variables. The t-test is designed to test for a possible significant difference in the means of two groups (or two time periods for the same group) where one variable is nominal and one the other is an interval level variable. Both correlation coefficients and multiple regression are designed to test for relationships between interval level variables. We will consider the meaning and use of each of these tools in this chapter.

Chi-Square

The purpose of the Chi-Square test is to determine if a relationship exists between two nominal variables. Based upon mathematical properties of the normal curve and the probability of statistical differences between observed and expected outcomes, i.e., the differences between what was observed in a particular study and what one would expect if there were no relationship between two variables, SPSS utilizes the appropriate Chi-Square formula for computing for the existence of a relationship. The actual mathematical theory behind this formula is beyond the scope of the present course, but the formula and a brief explanation of its use will be included in our discussion of Chi-Square.

The calculated value of the Chi-Square test statistic is compared to a critical Chi-Square value which corresponds to a desired level of probability that the differences in two variables of interest could have occurred by chance as opposed to inferring a causal association between the two variables. In other words, the Chi-Square test statistic is computed for the observed table and is then compared to the Chi-Square value required for an acceptable margin of error. If the obtained test statistic is greater than the required value, then a relationship is said to be observed between the two nominal level variables. The standard level of probability in social science is the ".05" level. In lay terminology, the ".05" level of probability corresponds to a "margin of error" of 5% (multiply .05 x 100 in order to obtain a percentage). If a test statistic is "within the acceptable level of probability or margin of error," then the researcher concludes that the pattern being observed in the data is real. How sure can she be that there is an actual relationship and not one occurring by mere chance? She can be 95% certain that the observed relationship is real. The risk of this conclusion being in error is only 5% (100% - 5% margin of error = 95%).

If the value of the obtained Chi-Square test statistic is less than the critical value required for the .05 level, then the researcher concludes that there is no statistically significant relationship between the two variables. There may be variation observed, but the variation is not great enough to warrant our conclusion that the independent variable is responsible for this change, i.e., it may be occurring by chance. Alternately, the independent variable may have some influence on the dependent variable, but there may be many other factors responsible for changes in the dependent variable as well, which weaken the appearance of a association between the two variables.

The formula for computing the Chi-Square test statistic is:

$$\text{CHI-SQUARE} = \text{SUM}[(O - E)^2 / E]$$

O = the observed frequency in the cell of a table
E = the expected frequency in the cell if no relationship exists

Expected frequencies are calculated for each cell as follows:

$$E = [(\text{row marginal})(\text{column marginal})]/N$$

In other words, we determine the frequency expected for each cell if there were no relationship, find the difference between the expected and observed frequency and square this difference (for each cell), and finally add the squared differences for each cell together. The following example illustrates the process.

STUDENT STATUS

		Underclassmen	Upperclassmen	M
DRINKING	Slight	O = 8	O = 5	13
PROBLEM		E = $\frac{13 \times 14}{30}$ = 6.07	E = $\frac{13 \times 16}{30}$ = 6.93	
	Serious	O = 6	O = 11	17
		E = $\frac{17 \times 14}{30}$ = 7.93	E = $\frac{17 \times 16}{30}$ = 9.07	
M		14	16	30

In the above table, there are 8 underclassmen who have a slight drinking problem and 6 who have a serious one. There are 5 upperclassmen who have a slight drinking problem and 11 who have a serious problem. What can we conclude? We observe a greater proportion (or percentage, should we choose to calculate percentages for each cell of the table) of the upperclassmen have a serious drinking problem (11 out of 16, approximately two-thirds of the upperclassmen) then the underclassmen (6 our of 14, less than half of the underclassmen). We can report these findings because this is what we are finding in the sample studied. The statistical question now becomes: to what extent are these observed differences by student status statistically significant, i.e., can we be sure that these differences are not occurring by chance, but are really the outcome of a relationship (becoming an upperclassman increases one's chances becoming a problem drinker)?

Let's use the Chi-Square formula to obtain the test statistic:

Chi-Square =

$$(8\text{-}6.07)^2/6.07 + (5\text{-}6.93)^2/6.93 + (6\text{-}7.93)^2/7.93 + (11\text{-}9.07)^2/9.07$$

$$= .62 + .54 + .47 + .41 = \underline{2.04}$$

In a Chi-Square test there are, by definition, $(r\text{-}1)(c\text{-}1)$ degrees of freedom (df). What are degrees of freedom? The mathematical properties which determine df are beyond the scope of this course. Suffice it to say that number theory stipulates the size of the required Chi-Square value varies with the size of the table, i.e., the number of cells in the table. Therefore, when computing significance levels we need to adjust for the number of cells in the table. By definition the size is always one less than the number of rows, "r," multiplied by one less than the number of columns, "c," or df = $(r\text{-}1)(c\text{-}1)$. In the example above, we have what is called a "2 by 2 table." There are two rows and two columns. A "2x3 table" would have two rows and three columns. A "3x3 table" contains three rows and three columns. A "3x4 table" contains three rows and four columns. Returning to the above example, a 2X2 table contains one degree of freedom (df = 1). Why? The df for a 2x2 table:

$$df = (r\text{-}1)(c\text{-}1) = (2\text{-}1)(2\text{-}1) = (1)(1) = 1$$

Before we had computers to do this work for us we had to compute chi-square test statistics and degrees of freedom ourselves. We would then use a standard chi-square distribution table to determine if our computed chi-square was significant at the .05 level. For example, returning to our earlier computations we have computed our Chi-Square test statistic, 2.04, and we have computed our degrees of freedom, df = 1. We would now determine if our chi-square value was significant at the .05 level of probability. To do this we must turn to a standard Chi-Square Critical Values Table--you have probably followed this procedure in math courses you have had. First you would find the ".05" column and the df row for 1 df. Where these two intersect in the Critical Values Table you would find the required value for the chi-square test statistic to be statistically significant (within our required margin of error of 5%). I located a critical values table and found that a critical value of 3.841 given. What does this mean?

Chi-Square test statistic = 2.04
Chi-Square critical value = 3.841

2.04 < 3.841

No Relationship Observed in Data

The obtained chi-square test statistic is less than the critical value required for our standard margin of error. Therefore, we conclude that there is not a statistically significant difference between drinking patterns (slight versus serious) of upper versus underclassmen. There may be an observed difference, but it does not vary enough for us to be sure (at least 95% of the time) that it is the result of a true relationship as opposed to a chance occurrence. So we conclude that these small differences observed in our sample are the result of chance.

Interpreting a Table and Applying Chi-Square to the Report. Let's return to our "Student Alcohol Survey." Let's assume that one research question in our Alcohol Study was: "Does incidence of drinking problems vary by gender?" Hence, we are interested in comparing two variables, gender (independent variable) and existence of drinking problems (dependent variable). Sex is a nominal variable while Freq and Amount are both ordinal level variables. Either Freq or Amount could be used as an indicator of a drinking problem (frequency of drinking episodes versus amount consumed per sitting). Regardless of which variable we choose, we need to recode it into two sub-categories: drinking problem versus no drinking problem. We would also, of course, have to decide how to operationally define drinking problem and recode accordingly. The next step is to use the computer crosstabulate our variables and provide us with the chi-square test results. Let's try it. Here is an example of what we might find (notice how the table is set up, use it as a model for your own work):

TABLE 3   THE IMPACT OF GENDER ON DRINKING PATTERNS

	SEX	
DRINKING PROBLEM	Male	Female
Yes	57%	31%
No	43%	69%
	100%	100%
	(70)	(80) N = 150

Chi-Square = 4.52   df = 1   Significance = .042

How do we read the above table? Well, a majority of males (57%) have a drinking problem while a majority of females (69%) do not. Is this difference large enough (in opposite directions) for us to conclude that gender plays a role in determining one's chances of developing a drinking problem? According to the chi-square results we can conclude that gender is associated with drinking behavior in some way. [Perhaps gender role socialization will help us sociologically explain why this pattern is observed.] How do I reach this conclusion? The significance level of this chi-square test statistic is .042 which is less than the required .05 level of significance meaning that we can conclude (within a 5% margin of error) that this observed pattern did not occur by chance. In other words, these two variables are associated with one another. In the above table the chi-square test statistic, degrees of freedom and computed level of significance are included. When constructing your own table for your report, follow this pattern. When you use SPSS to obtain such a table and the chi-square test statistic it provides the actual level of significance. By examining the computer generated level of significance you automatically know if this table's chi-square is greater or less than the required .05 level.

How does one report these chi-square findings? Actually we simply add a sentence or two to what we have already written when we were writing up our crosstabulated tables (in Chapter 3). Now, instead of indicating that there appears to be a relationship or not, we use the chi-square results to clearly state that there is or is not a statistically significant difference between what is going on between the independent and dependent variables. And, we interpret the meaning of what is observed.

There are really only four possible outcomes. (1) Using gender and drinking as an example, one gender may be drinking so much more than the other that we find a statistically significant difference between the drinking behavior of each gender. (2) Another possible outcome is if there is only a small difference between drinking by gender, so small a difference that it is not a statistically significant one and, therefore, we consider the drinking of men and women to be the same. (3) Alternately, we may find that a majority of both men and women are drinking to the same extent--no significant difference in their behavior. And, (4) we may find that even though both genders are drinking, say, allot, the men are drinking so much that it is still a significant difference in comparison to the women. We need to see examples of each of these.

Possible Outcome #1

Clearly a relationship exists between gender and incidence of drinking problems. Approximately two-thirds of the men (69%) exhibited a tendency toward having a drinking problem, while less than a third of the women (31%) demonstrated the same. The observed relationship between gender and drinking is a statistically significant one (Chi-Square=4.52, df=1, sig.=.042, please see Table 3). Men are found to be more likely to develop a drinking problem than women.

TABLE 3   THE IMPACT OF GENDER ON DRINKING PATTERNS

		SEX	
DRINKING PROBLEM		Male	Female
	Yes	69%	31%
	No	31%	69%
		100%	100%
Chi-Square = 4.52	df = 1	Significance = .04	

Notice how the parameters of the relationship are described in clear technical language that is easy for the reader to understand, rather than rambling on and on from one percentage to another. The relevant percentages are included within parentheses at the appropriate time. A clear statement is made with respect to whether or not the observed relationship is statistically significant. The specific supporting data is provided parenthetically, along with a reference for the reader to know what table to refer to if she wants to take a closer look at the table herself (thus the "please see Table 3" reference). And, a final interpretation of the meaning of the observed relationship is provided.

In the previous example it was easy to interpret what the trends are by gender and the chi-square test statistic. You will be lucky when you come across findings that are so nice and tidy in their obvious interpretation. Most social research does not result in such clarity. In fact, most of the data you analyze will not result in a statistically significant relationship. So, be prepared for reality! In order to prepare you for the researcher's reality, let's consider writing samples of each of the other three possible options you might find in your data.

Possible Outcome #2

A majority of men (54%) report a drinking problem while a majority of women (52%) do not. The difference is so small, however, so that this pattern has not been found to be a statistically significant one (Chi-Square = 3.01, df = 1, sig. = .095). We conclude that there is no difference in drinking behavior on the basis of gender.

TABLE 3   THE IMPACT OF GENDER ON DRINKING PATTERNS

		SEX	
DRINKING PROBLEM		Male	Female
	Yes	54%	48%
	No	46%	52%
		100%	100%
Chi-Square = 3.01		df = 1	Significance = .09

Possible Outcome #3

No relationship was observed between income and incidence of drinking alcoholic beverages. Two-thirds (68%) of the wealthier respondents do not have a drinking problem, almost two-thirds (65%) of the middle income respondents do not, and exactly two-thirds (67%) of the lower income respondents do not drink at a problematic level. There is no statistically significant difference observed (chi-square = 1.54, df = 2, sig. = .889). Income does not impact on drinking behavior.

TABLE 3   THE IMPACT OF GENDER ON DRINKING PATTERNS

		SEX	
DRINKING PROBLEM		Male	Female
	Yes	32%	35%
	No	68%	65%
		100%	100%
Chi-Square = 1.01		df = 1	Significance = .89

Possible Outcome #4

> Gender has been found to impact on drinking behavior in the current study. Most of the men (98%) developed a drinking problem, while a bare majority of women (53%) did the same. The observed pattern was found to be a statistically significant one (chi-square = 25.68, df = 1, sig. = .03). Men have been found to be far more likely then women to develop a drinking problem.

TABLE 3   THE IMPACT OF GENDER ON DRINKING PATTERNS

		SEX	
DRINKING PROBLEM		Male	Female
	Yes	32%	35%
	No	68%	65%
		100%	100%
Chi-Square = 1.01	df = 1	Significance = .89	

Using SPSS to Obtain Chi-Square Test Results. Working from the spreadsheet of the data file of interest, select "Statistics," then "Summarize," followed by "Crosstabs," and select the dependent and independent variable as you have done before. Now the new twist: select "Statistics" and indicate which options you desire. You want to select "chi-square" and "contingency statistics." Don't forget to select "Cells" and compute "column" percentages. After indicating "OK," the crosstab table and chi-square test results will appear in your output window. Illustration V:1 summarizes these steps and Illustration V:2 provides an example of what the output will look like.

Illustration V:1   Chi-Square Test of Significance

Looking for Possible Association Between Two Variables:
Independent & Dependent Nominal or Ordinal Variables

Get the Crosstabs

Get the Spreadsheet of the Data File Up on Screen
Select Statistics
Select Summarize
Select Crosstabs
Determine which two variables you want to look at for a possible association
Determine which variable is the Dependent Variable
Move the Dependent Variable into the right box (rows)
Determine which variable is the Independent Variable
Move the Independent Variable into the right box (columns)
Select Desired Statistic (Chi-Square & Contingency Statistics)
Select Cells Box & Select Columns
OK

Viewing the Crosstabs

When Output Appears on Screen:
        Use up/down arrows to scroll thru output window
        Obtain print out of hard copy of crosstabs table(s) if desired
        Save Crosstabs table(s) in new file if desired

3. Reading Tables
Note Variables listed (I at top of table, D on left side)
Note value labels & numbers listed for each (top of each column and side of
        each row)
Read percentages DOWN the COLUMNS, they should sum to 100%, e.g., 75% of
        those having alcoholic parents are alcoholic while 25% are not; conversely
        (2nd column) 80% of those not having an alcoholic parent are not alcoholic
        (pattern!!!)
Note number of respondents in each cell too
Note the Chi-Square contingency coefficient (Chi-Square test statistic) is provided
        as well as level of significance (.01, .05., etc.)
Use significance level to determine if there is or is not an association between the
        two variables

Illustration V:2 Sample Chi-Square Output

```
FREQ1  recoded freq  by  SEX  gender

                          SEX              Page 1 of 1
                 Count
                 Col Pct |female  male
                                               Row
                         |   1.00|   2.00| Total
FREQ1           ─────────┼───────┼───────┤
                    1.00 |    6   |    2  |    8
         monthly or less |  50.0  |  20.0 |  36.4

                    2.00 |    6   |    8  |   14
         weekly or more  |  50.0  |  80.0 |  63.6

                  Column     12      10      22
                  Total     54.5    45.5   100.0

           Chi-Square              Value        DF        Significance

   Contingency Coefficient        .29656                   .14525 *1
```

T-Test

The t-test is designed to help the researcher determine if there is a statistically significant difference between the means of either (1) two sub-groups of a variable or (2) a group in two different time periods (detect change over time). For example, we may be interested in determining if women students consume, on average, a higher or lower number of drinks per evening when compared to their male counterparts. The t-test enables us to determine if the difference between the two groups, i.e., genders, is a statistically significant one. The t-test also enables us to compare pairs of respondents. For example, we may be interested to know if the consumption pattern is greater, lower or the same after completing a new campus-wide anti-alcohol campaign. In this case, information on drinking behavior would be gathered twice, before and after the anti-alcohol effort. We could then compare the drinking frequency in time 1 versus time 2 to see if the difference is a statistically significant one and thereby determine if the program is effective.

The mathematical computations and numbers theory that this statistical procedure is based upon is beyond the scope of the present course. A math statistics course usually provides this background. This book is directed toward the social science user who wants to focus on how to get the data from the questionnaire, into the computer, out of the computer in a useable form and then interpret this output as a social scientist. We will, therefore, provide only a brief overview of the mathematical essence of the t-test.

The t-test is based upon a principal of the normal curve which attempts to compare the variation of the means of two populations. The comparison examines the extent to which the individual responses of each group vary around the mean of each group and how this variation compares between the two groups. If the variance around the means differs significantly, then the conclusion the researcher derives is that the behavior varies significantly between the two groups (or two time periods for the same group).

Interpreting T-Test Results for 2 Groups. If we were to ask SPSS to give us the t-test results for the average drinking frequency by gender we might get a table that looks similar to the following one.

Group 1: Female   Group 2: Male

T-Test for: FREQ

	# of cases	Mean	Stand. Dev.	Error
Group 1	50	2.1	.8	.08
Group 2	48	5.3	.6	.98

F value: 1.6   Probability: .10

Equal Variance	t value: 1.78	Degrees of Freedom: 96	Probability: .078
Unequal	t value: 1.77	Degrees of Freedom: 89	Probability: .08

The interpretation of the t-test statistic is similar to how you have been interpreting chi-square. The key is the level of probability or margin of error, i.e., is the statistical computation yielding a margin of error of 5% or less? In the example in the above table, we find that there were 50 females in the current study and 48 men. The women reportedly consume an average of two drinks per evening while the men averaged five. Since the standard deviation for women is ".8" and is ".6" for men, we can conclude that two-thirds of the women drink between one and three drinks. Two-thirds of the men consume between five and six drinks.

In order to determine if there is a significant difference between the drinking frequency of men and women, we must decide which t-test statistic to use in the provided table. In order to make this decision we must first determine if the populations from which the samples are drawn are significantly different in size. This is done by use of the F value which is 1.6, in the current example, and has a probability of ".10." If the F value probability is equal to or less than ".05," we then conclude that the populations are not equal in size, and we use the unequal variance t-test statistic (there is a statistically significant difference in size between the two groups). If the F value probability is greater than ".05" we then use the equal variance t-test statistic because we conclude that the populations are approximately equal in size (no statistically significant difference) [population size will influence the computation of the t-test statistic and must be adjusted for by selecting the appropriate variance]. In the above

If F value significance is < or = .05, use Unequal Variance
(populations not equal, there is a statistically significant difference)
If F value significance is > .05, use Equal Variance
(populations are approximately equal, there is no significant difference)

example, the F value probability is greater than ".05" so we use the *equal variance t-test statistic*:

t-value: 1.78   probability: .078

Since the probability (.078) is greater than our acceptable margin of error (.05), we conclude that there is no statistically significant difference between the average drinking frequency of men and women in this sample. What does this mean to us sociologically? In this study gender did not prove to be an explanatory variable, i.e., an independent or causal variable.   Drinking frequency cannot be predicted on the basis of one's gender. Another variable(s) must be influencing one's drinking frequency.   Could it be the student subculture? Perhaps. Further research and data analysis is needed to answer this question.

Interpreting T-Test Results for Time1-Time2 Studies. In this case, the t-test value and probability will be easier to read. The results will appear in the output when SPSS used to compute the t-test for pairs or time studies. There is no use of an F value. Merely interpret the results based upon the designated probability, i.e., if it is equal to or less than ".05" there is a significant difference between time1 and time2.   If the probability exceeds ".05" there is no difference in performance over time or between the paired respondents.

Language to Use When Writing With T-Test Statistics.   The following is an example of how one may write about the study's findings when using t-test statistics:

> One of the research questions under consideration in the present study is: to what extent does drinking vary by gender? The researchers hypothesized that men, on average, would consume alcoholic beverages more often then women. The findings, however, suggest a different conclusion. We observed no statistically significant difference in the average drinking behavior of men versus women (t-value = 1.78, p = .078, please see table 3). Both men and women averaged approximately one evening out per week during which alcoholic beverages were consumed.

Table Presentation. The following format is the proper model to emulate when constructing a table to present t-test results. In this example the two groups are male and female (gender is the variable) and number of drinks consumed in a typical evening during which alcoholic beverages are served.

Table 3   Drinking Differences by Gender

Alcohol Consumption	N	Mean	t-test	p
Men	156	3	4.5	.04
Women	168	1		

Using SPSS to Obtain T-Test Results (for two groups). Operating from the spreadsheet environment of the desired data file, select "Statistics," then "Compare Means," and choose the "Independent" test. Select the desired variables for the t-test to be computed for and identify the group values for the group variable, e.g., gender. After indicating "OK" the computations will appear in the output window. Illustration V:3 summarizes these steps and Illustration V:4 provides an example of t-test output.

Using SPSS to Obtain T-Test Results (for Time1-Time2). Operating from the spreadsheet environment of the desired data file, select "Statistics," then "Compare Means," and choose the "Pairs" test. Select the desired variables for the t-test, e.g., exam1 and exam2 to compare the differences between a pre-test and post-test for a classroom of students. After indicating "OK" the computations will appear in the output window. Again, Illustration V:3 summarizes these steps.

Illustration V:3   T-TESTS
Testing for Differences:
Groups & Pairs/Time1-Time2

Getting T-Test Results

Get Spreadsheet of Data File Up on Screen
Select Statistics
Select Compare Means
Choose the appropriate T-Test Option
    IF you want to compare Time 1 versus Time 2 on the same people
    (example: beginning salary versus current salary) to see if there is a
    statistically significant difference between then and now,
        THEN SELECT "PAIRS"
    IF you want to compare what is happening between two groups
    (example: men's versus women's beginning salary) to see if there is a
    statistically significant difference between their earnings,
        THEN SELECT "INDEPENDENT"
Select & Move desired variables to run t-test on to box (designate values in
    case of 2 groups, 0 for men and 1 for women)
OK

Viewing the T-Test Results

When Output Appears on screen:
    Use up/down arrows to scroll thru output window
    Obtain print out of hard copy of t-test results if desired
    Save results in lst (list) file if desired

Reading Tables

    a. <u>Pairs</u>
        note var names on left of table, e.g., SALBEG & SALNOW
        note number of pairs
        note means for each (average beginning salary and ave sal now)
        note t-value, df, and (most important) significance level
            (.05 or less means
        stat sig difference between salaries then and now)

    b. <u>Groups</u>
        note groups on left of table, e.g., males and females
        note number of cases in each group
        note means for each group (ave male salary then vs. ave
            female sal then)
        note t-value, df, and (most important) significance level
            (.05 or less??)
       Whose starting salary, on average, was more?
       Is the difference a statistically significant one?
       Would this finding support a hypothesis that salary discrimination
       exists/existed on the basis of gender (whereby men were paid
            more than women, JUST because they were male)?

Illustration V:4   Sample T-Test Output

```
t-tests for Independent Samples of SEX    GENDER
```

Variable	Number of Cases	Mean	SD	SE of Mean
SCORE RAPE MYTH SCORE				
MALE	46	60.6957	7.513	1.108
FEMALE	49	65.4490	6.341	.906

```
Mean Difference = -4.7533

Levene's Test for Equality of Variances: F= .790    P= .376
```

Variances	t-test for Equality of Means t-value	df	2-Tail Sig	SE of Diff	95% CI for Diff
Equal	-3.34	93	.001	1.423	(-7.580, -1.927)
Unequal	-3.32	88.30	.001	1.431	(-7.597, -1.910)

Analysis of Variance (ANOVA)

Analysis of Variance (One-Way ANOVA) enables the researcher to determine if there is a statistically significant difference between two or more means. The means (interval level variable) are compared for the various, two or more, categories of a nominal variable. When examining the difference in means between two groups or categories, we are really doing the same data analysis as we do with a t-test. The advantage of ANOVA comes when the researcher wants to compare the means of more than two groups of nominal categories.

Mathematical Meaning. ANOVA calculates the ratio of two variances. It compares the variance of each individual respondent's answer within the group with the group's mean to the variance of the difference between each group's mean with the overall mean. These variances are referred to as the *within* and *between* groups sums of squares. The *F distribution* is approximated (you should have been exposed to the properties of the F distribution in a math statistics course) by the ratio of the between and within variances. The total sums of squares is computed by:

Sum the Squared Differences of the Individual Values and the Overall Mean.

The number of degrees of freedom are determined by subtracting one from the sample size (n - 1). For example, if the sample size is 150, then the degrees of freedom for total sums of squares are 149 (150-1).

To determine the within-group sum of squares, we examine the variation between individual values around the respective group means. The degrees of freedom are computed as the total sample size minus the number of groups. For example, if the sample size (n) is 150 and if there are three groups (k), then the degrees of freedom are 147 (150 - 3).

To determine the between-groups sum of squares, we examine the variation of the group means around the overall mean. The degrees of freedom are determined by subtracting one from the number of groups. For example, if there are 3 groups, then the degrees of freedom are two (3 - 1).

Interpreting ANOVA. Let's work with an example. Suppose we gathered data which suggests that the average number of drinks consumed during a typical party is as follows:

Fraternity/Sorority Members   5.4 drinks
Varsity Athletes   6.8 drinks
All Other Students   3.1 drinks

Let's further suppose that one of our research tasks in the current example is to determine if there is a statistically significant difference in drinking behavior between the various groups. We could compute a t-test three separate times comparing each possible combination of the above three groups. Alternately, we could use one-way ANOVA to determine if there is a significant difference in the means of these three groups.

By using ANOVA we might obtain the following information from our computer when running SPSS Windows:

Source	Sums of Squares	df	Mean Squares	F	P
between	1,925	2	525	3.05	.01
within	4,567	147	1,456		
Total	6,492	149	2,145		

The significance level (.01 in this example) is less than our required level (.05). We conclude that there is a statistically significant difference between the means of the three groups. Hence, we can conclude that varsity athletes, and then fraternity and sorority members, are significantly more likely to consume larger amounts of alcohol at parties than other students. If the computed F-value significance had been greater than .05 then we would conclude that there is no significant difference in the drinking behaviors of the various groups. As far as we would be concerned they all consume the same amount.

Writing Sample.   Using the above example, let's examine an example of how to report these findings with the help of one-way ANOVA.

A statistically significant difference (F=3.05, df=2, p=.01) was observed between the drinking behavior of the groups of students under consideration. The varsity athletes were more likely to consume larger amounts of alcohol per party (mean number of drinks consumed = 7). Those affiliated with a Greek organization on campus were likely to consume less (5 drinks) than the athletes, but more than other students (who averaged 3 drinks per party). Please see Table 3.

Using SPSS to Obtain ANOVA.   Working from an SPSS spreadsheet, access the desired data file then select "Statistics," then select the menu option "Compare Means," followed by "One-Way ANOVA." At this point indicate which is the independent versus the dependent variable in the dialogue box. You must also specify the range of answer options. Select the desired statistics and options. Finally, activate the computation by selecting "OK." Output will appear in your output window for your perusal. Please refer to Illustrations V and VI for a summarized list of the steps and sample output.

Illustration V   Steps for Obtaining ANOVA via SPSS

Obtain SPSS Windows Spreadsheet
Obtain Desired Data File
Select "Statistics"
Select "Compare Means"
Select "One-Way ANOVA"
Indicate D and I variables
Indicate Range
Select Desired Statistics and Options
"OK"

Illustration VI   Sample SPSS ANOVA Output

- - - - - O N E W A Y - - - - -

Variable   SCORE   RAPE MYTH SCORE
By Variable   RELIGION   RELIGION

Analysis of Variance

Source	D.F.	Sum of Squares	Mean Squares	F Ratio	F Prob.
Between Groups	4	447.7839	111.9460	2.3185	.0653
Within Groups	71	3428.1503	48.2838		
Total	75	3875.9342			

Group	Count	Mean	Standard Deviation	Standard Error	95 Pct Conf Int for Mean		
PROTESTA	33	64.4242	6.0054	1.0454	62.2948	TO	66.5537
JEWISH	2	72.5000	3.5355	2.5000	40.7345	TO	104.2655
CATHOLIC	39	60.8974	7.7146	1.2353	58.3966	TO	63.3982
BUDDHIST	1	65.0000					
HINDU	1	68.0000					
Total	76	62.8816	7.1888	.8246	61.2389	TO	64.5243

GROUP	MINIMUM	MAXIMUM
PROTESTA	50.0000	76.0000
JEWISH	70.0000	75.0000
CATHOLIC	39.0000	79.0000
BUDDHIST	65.0000	65.0000
HINDU	68.0000	68.0000
TOTAL	39.0000	79.0000

Pearson Correlation Coefficients

The chi-square test statistic enables the researcher to determine if the observed relationship between two nominal level variables is statistically significant. It does not indicate the strength or direction of the observed relationship. The t-test provides the researcher with the opportunity to detect if there is a statistically significant difference between the behavior two groups (or pairs or time periods)--when one variable is nominal and the other is an interval level variable. It too does not indicate the strength or direction of the observed relationship. The Pearson correlation coefficient (r) does provide both additional pieces of information for the researcher. In order to use this statistical procedure, the two variables must both be **ungrouped interval level** variables (although if it is a grouped interval level variable or an ordinal variable which has enough categories, e.g., nine or more, then it can be treated as an ungrouped interval level variable for correlation test purposes). For example, if we obtain the actual age, income, number of years of education, test score, or IQ score, then we are working with an ungrouped interval level variable. The correlation coefficient is designed for ungrouped interval level variables. If there are enough income categories, as in the below example, one could still use the correlation coefficient:

(1) less than $10,000
(2) $10,000 thru $19,999
(3) $20,000 thru $29,999
(4) $30,000 thru $39,999
(5) $40,000 thru $49,999
(6) $50,000 thru $59,999
(7) $60,000 thru $69,999
(8) $70,000 thru $79,999
(9) $80,000 and above

The advantage of using the correlation coefficient is that it provides all three previously noted pieces of information, significance, strength, and direction.

Pearson Correlation Coefficient. The Pearson correlation coefficient, "r," is calculated by the computer on the basis of the following general formula:

$$r = \text{square root of (explained variance/total variance)}$$

This formula suggests that the correlation coefficient is large when the numerator is large, i.e., the variation between the two variables is large-- a change in one causes a large change in the other. Further mathematical details are beyond the scope of this course. It is necessary for you to understand the general nature of what "r" means, however.

Direction. The computed correlation coefficient, or "r," ranges from a possible " -1.0 " to a possible " +1.0 ". The sign, negative or positive indicates the direction of the relationship, i.e., a negative or positive direction. A negative "r" means that an increase in the independent variable is associated with a decrease in the dependent variable. Suppose we found that the more people use seat belts, the lower the number of traffic fatalities. The previous relationship is an inverse or negative one, i.e., an increase in the independent variable (seat belt wearing) results in a decrease in the dependent variable (traffic fatalities). The correlation coefficient would be negative.

A positive "r" means that an increase in the independent variable results in an increase in the dependent variable. Suppose we found that more years of formal education results in higher starting salaries. This relationship would be a direct or positive one.

If the correlation coefficient were neither positive nor negative, but neutral, i.e., a zero (r = 0.0), then there is absolutely no relationship observed between the two variables, an increase or decrease in the independent variable results in no increase or decrease in the dependent variable.

Strength. The strength of the relationship is indicated by how close the correlation coefficient is to the integer (positive or negative) " 1.0 " versus " 0.0 ". The closer the "r" value is to +/- 1.0, the stronger the relationship, be it a direct (positive) relationship or an inverse (negative) relationship. The strongest possible positive relationship is "r = 1.0," (or -1.0) which means that the "I" (independent variable) is solely responsible for the "D" (dependent variable), i.e., any change in one results in change in the other. Conversely, the closer the "r" value is to 0.0, the weaker the relationship is found to be. And, if "r = 0.0," there is no relationship, i.e., changes in "I" do not cause or explain any change in "D". The following guide is offered to help the researcher interpret the meaning of the "r" values so that she can clearly communicate the strength of the relationships when reporting the findings.

Pearson Correlation Coefficient Guide

If r = +/- 0.8 to 1.0	very strong relationship
If r = +/- 0.6 to 0.79	strong relationship
If r = +/- 0.4 to 0.59	moderately strong relationship
If r = +/- 0.2 to 0.39	moderately weak relationship
If r = +/- 0.0 to 0.19	very weak/no relationship

Significance Levels. Do you remember what we said earlier about significance levels, i.e., margins of error? If not, please turn back to our chi-square discussion of levels of significance. Everything discussed about significance levels earlier in this book applies to correlation coefficients as well. Our standard rule of thumb is that the observed relationship must be found to be occurring at the ".05" level or lower, otherwise the observed relationship is assumed to be occurring by chance rather than being a true causal relationship.

Interpreting Correlation Coefficients. SPSS Windows will provide you with correlation data which will look similar to the following example:

	AGE	YRSED	TIMES	DRINKS
AGE	1.000	.876	-.433	-.566
	(167)	(167)	(167)	(167)
	P =.	P = .01	P = .05	P = .05
YRSED	.876	1.000	-.543	-.654
	(167)	(167)	(167)	(167)
	P = .05	P =.	P = .05	P = .05
TIMES	-.433	-.543	1.000	.889
	(167)	(167)	(167)	(167)
	P = .05	P = .05	P =.	P = .001
DRINKS	-.566	-.654	.889	1.000
	(167)	(167)	(167)	(167)
	P = .05	P = .05	P = .001	P =.

We must first interpret what these numbers mean. The first line under a variable name is the correlation coefficient. The second line contains the number of respondents in the study. The third line contains the level of significance (the "P = " refers to probability of error). In the above table it will seem to the neophyte researcher that correlation coefficients must always be pretty strong and statistically significant. Nothing could be further from the truth in the real world of social research. Remember that the data used in this chapter is fictional and provided only to illustrate the process of interpretation and use.

Let's interpret the above. You will notice that each relationship is within our margin of error (5%). You can conclude that each observed relationship is statistically significant, i.e., not occurring in the sample by mere chance. However, we only consider the relationships in the table that we need to use to help us answer the research question. Therefore, we do not use every combination of variables provided by the computer. And, the first question to ask oneself when examining such a table is "which pairs of variables are statistically significant?" Whenever a relationship is not statistically significant the strength and direction are irrelevant.

How about the direction and strength of each relationship? As a rule of thumb, look for the strongest relationship in the table and discuss it first, then proceed down to the weaker ones. With this model in mind, we find that the strongest relationship is the one between drinking frequency and the average amount of alcohol consumed in a given sitting. The correlation coefficient, is ".889" which is a "very strong relationship" according to our correlation coefficient interpretation guide provided earlier. What is the direction of this relationship? Well, the ".889" is positive, not negative, hence we conclude that it is a direct relationship. In other words, the greater the incidence of going out to party, the greater the amount of alcohol consumed on any given occasion. Let's pause for a moment to consider what this means. Frequent drinkers, in our study, were found to consume more every time they do drink then those who rarely drink. Understand? [If not, see your professor!]

Our research question (What impacts on drinking behavior?) directs us to determine if age and the number of years of formal education impact on the number of times the respondent goes out to drink and the number of drinks consumed during an evening. What is the nature of the observed relationship between education and number of drinks consumed? It is a statistically significant one, it is inverse and it is rather strong (r = -.654, s = .05). What does this mean? The greater the number of years of formal education completed, the less likely one is to consume allot of alcohol. Do you see how the correlation coefficient is a useful tool for helping the researcher explain what is going on in "the real world?" We would next examine the nature of the relationship between age and drinking, education and frequency of going out to party, and age and party frequency. Why in this order? First we determine if there is significance; we then report in the order of strength, i.e., strongest to weakest.

Report Language and Table Format. Remember that you are trying to communicate with a reader who is not familiar with your work. Strive to communicate as clearly as possible. At the same time, we use the appropriate technical language that creates a mental picture for the reader. The following is one example of how this is done. The research question in this example is: Under what conditions do students usually obtain a job in the shortest amount of time?

Being Pro-Active Pays

Contacting Employers Directly. The number of prospective employers the job seeker contacted to in person to submit a resume (after determining a position actually existed or would in the near future) was found to be strongly related to the speed with which a job was obtained. A strong statistically significant, inverse relationship (r = -.845, s = .001; please see Table 3) was observed. The greater the number of in-person contacts, the less time it took to obtain the desire position.

Not Waiting for the Job Advertisement. The time it takes to obtain a position was found to be greatly diminished when the job seeker did the leg work to determine where the jobs were--without waiting for ads to appear. A strong statistically significant, inverse relationship (r = -.823, s = .001) was observed between telephoning prospective employers to identify job opportunities and the length of time it took to obtain such a position. Calling to identify upcoming positions led to a quicker hire.

Networking Pays. When job seekers frequently told others about the search this helped to reduce the amount of time spent looking for employment--contacts were often suggested. A strong statistically significant, inverse relationship (r = -.788, s = .001) was observed between networking and the time it took to obtain a position. The more one networks, the sooner they are apt to find employment.

Education Rewards

Formal Education. The amount of formal education one attains does pay off in the job market. A moderately strong, statistically significant, inverse relationship (r = -.655, s = .04) was observed between education and the time it took to obtain a position.

Little or No Reward

Mass Mailings and Newspaper Ads of Little Help Mass Mailings of Resumes. Indiscriminately mailing resumes to every employer in the area had a negative impact on job seeking. A statistically significant, weak relationship existed between the number of such activities and the time it took to obtain a position (r = .223, s = .050). In other words, the more time devoted to such mass mailings, the longer it took to succeed in finding a position--a failed strategy!

The Impotence of Newspaper Ads. While such advertisements should never be ignored, their viability of their use as a primary strategy for finding a professional position is certainly called into question. No statistically significant relationship was observed (r = .125, s = .602). Apparently networking, and so forth, pay far richer dividends for the job seeker.

Table 3   Correlates of Success & Failure in the Job Search

	Network	Contact	Phone	Educ	Resume	News
Job	-.788*	-.845*	-.823*	-.655*	.223*	.125

* denotes statistical significance at .05 level or lower

Obtaining Correlation Coefficients Using SPSS Windows. Working from the spreadsheet environment of the data file of interest, select "Statistics," then select "Correlation," followed by "Bivariate." Indicate the variables for which you want to compute correlation coefficients and they will be computed and displayed in the output window after selecting "OK." Illustration V:7 provides a summary of these steps and Illustration V:8 is an example of what the output looks like.

Illustration V:7   Correlation Coefficients
Interval Level Data

Getting the Correlation Coefficients

Get the Spreadsheet of Data File Up on Screen
Select Statistics
Select Correlation
Select Bivariate
Select & Move Vars desire to look for relationships among
OK

Viewing the Correlation Coefficients

When Output Appears on Screen:
    Use the up/down arrows to scroll thru output window
    Obtain print out of hard copy of correlation coefficients if desired
    Save in lst (list) file if desired

Reading Tables

Note each variable appears twice: columns and rows first number in column is "r"
    (Pearson Correlation Coefficient) which assesses direction and strength of
    possible relationship second number in column is "n" (# of respondents) third
    number in column is "s" (statistical probability of their being a relationship,
    e.g., .05 or less rule of thumb)

Note: look at probability (s) first to determine if a relationship
    exists, then if one does, decide direction and strength

Illustration V:8   Correlation Output

```
              - -  Correlation Coefficients  - -

           AGE       SCORE     SEXEXP    SEXFRUST    SEXDRIVE    SICK

AGE       1.0000     .1786       .         .1100     -.2457      .0035
         (  101)    (   94)    (   18)    (  101)    (   18)    (  100)
         P-  .      P-  .085   P-  .      P-  .274   P-  .326   P-  .973

SCORE      .1786    1.0000       .         .5078      .1130      .2555
         (   94)    (   95)    (   18)    (   95)    (   18)    (   95)
         P-  .085   P-  .      P-  .      P-  .000   P-  .655   P-  .012

SEXEXP       .         .       1.0000       .          .          .
         (   18)    (   18)    (   18)    (   18)    (   18)    (   18)
         P-  .      P-  .      P-  .      P-  .      P-  .      P-  .

SEXFRUST   .1100      .5078       .        1.0000      .4486      .2832
         (  101)    (   95)    (   18)    (  102)    (   18)    (  101)
         P-  .274   P-  .000   P-  .      P-  .      P-  .062   P-  .004

SEXDRIVE  -.2457      .1130       .         .4486     1.0000      .2094
         (   18)    (   18)    (   18)    (   18)    (   18)    (   18)
         P-  .326   P-  .655   P-  .      P-  .062   P-  .      P-  .404

SICK       .0035      .2555       .         .2832      .2094     1.0000
         (  100)    (   95)    (   18)    (  101)    (   18)    (  101)
         P-  .973   P-  .012   P-  .      P-  .004   P-  .404   P-  .
```

(Coefficient / (Cases) / 2-tailed Significance)

" . " is printed if a coefficient cannot be computed

MULTIPLE REGRESSION

The Pearson correlation coefficient enables the researcher to determine the nature, strength and the level of significance for the relationship between a single independent and a single dependent variable. While it is a very useful tool, there are usually several causal variables that contribute to the creation of a behavior or circumstance in the world we are trying to better understand through our social research. Hence, it is often more desireable to think in terms of an explanatory model in which the impact of each of the various identified independent variables is individually and collectively assessed. Let's say, for example, that we would like to know the relative influence of age, years of education, and so forth, on drinking behavior. In other words, we are seeking to answer the following research question:

> Does drinking frequency and the amount of alcohol one consumes on a
> given occasion vary by the age, years of education, and income?

The statistical tool known as multiple regression is the method by which we can assess the individual and collective impact of a series of independent variables upon a given dependent variable. This section of the book will explain regression, demonstrate how to use this tool, how to use SPSS for multiple regression calculations, how to interpret what you get from SPSS, and how to report on your multiple regression findings.

Linear Regression. The researcher seeks to describe, explain and predict behavior patterns. The regression equation is a mathematically based attempt to facilitate the researcher's desire to accomplish these tasks. Based upon the least squares principle, the regression line is that which is formed by drawing a line through the plotted data which is the least distance from the data points. The regression equation is:

$$Y = a + bX + error$$

where Y = the value of the dependent variable
where a = the point at which the regression line crosses the y-axis
where b = the slope of the regression line
where X = the value of the independent variable
error = the margin of error

Linear regression, of course, assumes that if there is a relationship between the two variables in question, it is a linear one, i.e., as the independent variable increases in quantity then there is an accompanying increase (or decrease) in the quantity of the dependent variable.

Multiple Regression. Multiple regression is merely an expansion of linear regression in that instead of comparing one independent variable with a dependent variable, the researcher is comparing two or more independent variables, at the same time, with the dependent variable. Imagine, if you will, several regression lines being constructed across several planes of data. The multiple regression formula is, therefore:

$$Y = a + b_1 X_1 + b_2 X_2 + b_3 X_3 + \ldots (+ \text{ error})$$

the succeeding bX's represent the multiple slopes and independent variables in the model of multiple I variables

The objective in building a multiple regression model is to identify those variables which explain the variation in the dependent variable. The researcher strives to find those variables which account for most of the variation in the D variable. The general rule of thumb is to find the fewest independent variable(s) which explain the most variation in the dependent variable in order to obtain the best model.

Multiple Regression Coefficients. When you obtain a table of regression coefficients from the computer you normally obtain statistical information that looks like the below example:

VARIABLES IN THE EQUATION WITH DRINK

Variable	B	SE B	Beta	Significance
AGE	.052	.018	.142	.05
INCOME	.103	.013	.337	.01
YRSED	.031	.001	.592	.01
(CONSTANT)	3.391			

In the above table there are three items that are important to you: the variables, Beta values, and significance. In the current example DRINK (the Dependent variable) refers to the frequency of drinking reported by the respondent, AGE refers to the age of the student respondent, INCOME is the annual family income, and YRSED is number of years of completed formal education [Constant is not a variable, it is a statistical configuration that you need not concern yourself with as this is beyond the scope of this course.]

The Beta values are approximately analogous to the correlation coefficients you previously worked with, the primary difference being that they are adjusted for interaction with the other independent variables, i.e., the Beta value may be slightly smaller than an "r" because "I" variables do often have a causal influence upon one another. The significance level tells you if the observed Beta value is within the acceptable margin of error (5% or less). In the above example all are within the standard social science margin of error (.05). The Beta values are also called "Multiple R's" in other tables provided by SPSS.

R SQUARE. When you square the Multiple R, the obtained statistic represents the proportion of variation explained in the dependent variable by the examined independent variable. For example, in the above table the Beta (or Multiple R) for the relationship between YRSED and DRINK is .592 resulting in an "R Squared" (simply square the Multiple R) of .35. To obtain the percentage of variation in DRINK explained by YRSED, multiply the R Squared by 100:

$$\% \text{ Variation} = \text{R Squared} \times 100 = .35 \times 100 = 35\%$$

In other words, the percentage of variation in DRINK explained by YRSED is 35%, i.e., the amount of education one has completed impacts upon the drinking behavior (explains 35% of the variation).

Model Building Through Step-Wise Regression. Through the use of SPSS the researcher can easily build a regression model which identifies the variables which explain the most variation in the dependent variable. The researcher can compare all the relevant independent variables with the dependent variable and remove those which contribute a minimal explanation of variation, e.g., less than 1%. All of the independent variables are collectively compared with the "D" variable to determine the percentage of variance explained. Each variable (beginning with the one yielding the smallest percentage of variance explanation) is removed from the model. Your job as a researcher is to identify and keep those "I" variables which contribute the most to explaining the response in the "D" variable.

Sample Output. The following table is similar to the output you will obtain when you run multiple regression. Examine it closely, remember the key items for you include "I" and "D" variable names, the Multiple R, R Square, Beta values, and significance levels. When there is one "I" variable then the Multiple R and Beta value should be the same, when there are more two or more "I" variables the Multiple R represents the combined impact of the two "I" variables on the "D" variable (the Beta for "I" variable number one and "I" variable number two). The same principle applies to the R Square as well.

VARIABLE LIST: STEP WISE REGRESSION MODEL
DEPENDENT VARIABLE: DRINK

VARIABLES INCLUDED IN STEP ONE: AGE   INCOME   YRSED
MULTIPLE R   .7829
R SQUARE   .6130

VARIABLES IN THE EQUATION

VARIABLE	B	SE B	BETA	SIG
AGE	.052	.010	.1412	.01
INCOME	.099	.009	.3223	.01
YRSED	.031	.001	.5917	.01
(CONSTANT)	.999	.028		

VARIABLES INCLUDED IN STEP TWO: INCOME   YRSED
MULTIPLE R   .7706
R SQUARE   .5939

VARIABLES IN THE EQUATION

VARIABLE	B	SE B	BETA	SIG
INCOME	.094	.010	.3059	.01
YRSED	.002	.056	.6132	.01
(CONSTANT)	.001	.023		

VARIABLES INCLUDED IN STEP THREE: YRSED
MULTIPLE R   .5618
R SQUARE   .3156

VARIABLES IN THE EQUATION

VARIABLE	B	SE B	BETA	SIG
YRSED	.029	.001	.5618	.01
(CONSTANT)	.445	.022		

In the above example, all three variables explain quite a bit of variation in the dependent variable. In step one we have included age, income, and education which collectively explain 61.3% of the variation in drinking behavior. In step two we have excluded age, keeping income and education which explain 59.4% of the variation.

In other words, age explained (61.3% - 59.4% =) 1.9% of the variation in drinking. If it explains only one or two percent, we may want to drop it from our model. In step three we excluded both age and income, keeping only education which explains 31.56% of the variation in drinking. Our model should ultimately include both income and education as they explain large amounts of the variation in drinking behavior--only age does not. We conclude that education and income have a major impact on drinking.

Report Language. When constructing tables to report the Multiple Regression statistics follow the format outlined above. The language format for writing your research report findings involving the Multiple Regression model is exemplified below. An excellent source for more examples is the *American Sociological Review* which is published bimonthly by the American Sociological Association. It is found in the library.

> The appropriate Multiple Regression model for the examined data includes three independent variables: the amount of formal education completed during one's life and one's annual family income. We found that those who were better education were more likely to consume alcohol frequently then those who were not (beta = .5917, sig = .01). Furthermore, we found that those with higher family incomes were more likely to consume alcoholic beverages than those with lower incomes (beta = .3223, sig = .01). These two independent variables account for approximately 59% of the variation in drinking frequency, obviously they are major explanatory variables to be considered when predicting the circumstances under which one consumes alcoholic beverages. Our Multiple Regression Model is as follows:

> Drinking Frequency = YRS EDUC + INCOME

Notice how the writer attempts to paint a picture that is easy to understand, yet completely describes the important relationships by including the relevant information from the regression analysis. The complete statistical details are included in the table so that any reader can examine all the details to his or her satisfaction. Can you do this? It's time to find out! Does this mean it's homework time?

Obtaining Multiple Regression Output Using SPSS Windows. Let's try something different. I've been showing you how to use SPSS to obtain output for each statistical procedure, until now! There are other useful statistical procedures not included in this book, but which you may want to teach yourself. To prepare you for that eventuality, I would like you to teach yourself how to obtain multiple regression data. How? Why not return to the SPSS tutorial? You can also use the SPSS manual available in your computer lab as well as through your university book store. Good luck and I hope it turns out to be fun!

APPLICATION QUESTIONS

Chi-Square

1. If the computed Chi-Square test statistic is 8.67, and the degrees of freedom are two, significance = .04.   Is the relationship a statistically significant one? Explain.

2. If the computed Chi-Square is 10.82, d.f. = 1, significance = .001. Is this a statistically significant relationship? Explain.

3. Using the correct writing style, explain what is going on in the following data:

STUDENT DRINKING PATTERNS: Influenced by Class Standing?

CLASS

DRINKING FREQ	Underclassmen	Upperclassmen
Often	20%	45%
Sometimes	30%	40%
Never	50%	15%
Totals	100%	100%

Chi-Square = 228   d.f. = 2   sig. = .01

T-Test

4. If the t-value is 1.89 and the probability is .042, is there a statistically significant difference observed between the mean blue collar worker salaries and mean white collar worker salaries over their working life? Explain why you say yes or no.

5. If the F value is 2.6 and the probability is .04, do you use the equal or unequal variance t-value and significance? Explain.

6. The research question is: Do salaries differ significantly between blue collar workers and white collar workers? Explain using the below data.

T-Test for: SALARY

	# Cases	Mean	S.D.	Error
Blue Collar	542	$28,000	$2,000	142
White Collar	755	$42,000	$5,000	223

F value   = 1.8   probability = .04

Equal Variance
t value = 2.01 degrees of freedom 1295   probability = .09
Unequal Variance
t value = 1.87 degrees of freedom 1289   probability = .012

ANOVA

7. If the F value is 5.67, the degrees of freedom are 35, and the p = .05, is there a statistically significant difference between the means of the groups? Explain.

8. If the F value is 6.78, the degrees of freedom are 45, and the p = .09, is there a statistically significant difference between the means of the groups? Explain.

9. Using proper reporting language, analyze the following.

Sociology/Anthropology Majors	3.1 Mean GPA
Education Majors	3.4 Mean GPA
Math Majors	2.7 Mean GPA

Source	Sums of Squares	df	Mean Squares	F	P
between	2,925	2	525	5.12	.04
within	5,567	147	1,456		
Total	8,492	149	2,145		

Correlation

10. If the correlation coefficient is .45 and the probability is equal to .0448:
    (a) is the relationship significant and/or
    (b) does it have any strength?

11. If education and income are compared, with $r = .89$, $p = .001$, then what is the nature of the relationship between these two variables? Explain, using the appropriate writing style/language.

12. Use the below table to answer these two research questions.

    (a) Does one's formal education influence earning potential?
    (b) What variables impact on earning potential, note importance from greatest to lowest?

	EDUCATION	JOB YEARS	WORK ATTITUDE
EDUCATION	1.000	.224	.456
	(284)	(284)	(284)
	P =	P = .05	P = .01
JOB YEARS	.224	1.000	.331
	(284)	(284)	(284)
	P = .05	P =.	P = .05
WORK ATT.	.456	.331	1.000
	(284)	(284)	(284)
	P = .01	P = .05	P =.
SALARY	.89	.75	.67
	(284)	(284)	(284)
	P = .01	P = .01	P = .01

Multiple Regression

13. If the Multiple R is equal to .556, then what is the percentage of variation explained by the independent variable(s)?

14. The R Square for "I" Variable #1 is .667, the R Square for "I" Variables #1 & #2 together is .815, and the R Square for "I" Variables #1 & #2 & #3 together is .819. What is the best multiple regression model suggested by these data? Why?

15. The research question is: What variables explain the salary one receives on the job? Use the multiple regression model to answer this research question-- make sure to use the appropriate writing style/language. Use the data provided below.

DEPENDENT VARIABLE: SALARY

VARIABLES INCLUDED IN STEP ONE:		EDUCATION
MULTIPLE R	.889	YEARS ON JOB
R SQUARE	.790	WORK ATTITUDE

VARIABLES IN THE EQUATION

VARIABLE	B	SE B	BETA	SIG
EDUCATION	.188	.223	.389	.01
JOB YEARS	.177	.211	.300	.01
WORK ATT.	.089	.199	.200	.01
(CONSTANT)	.001	.028		

LAB SESSIONS

Session V:1
Chi-Square (In-Class Lab)

Access the appropriate data in order to complete the below lab activity. Do any necessary recoding (following recodes previously used when applicable). You may have to use "select if" sometimes. Use the correct writing language to state whether or not there are statistically significant relationships. Meet briefly with your professor after completing the first one below. E-mail the results for the other two when finished.

a:\StuAlco
Does drinking behavior vary by gender or class standing?

a:\Homework
Does academic performance vary by gender, study habits, or major?

s:\Alco
Does drinking behavior vary by gender, class standing, GPA, or drink preference?

Session V:2
Chi-Square (Homework Lab)

Obtain the appropriate Chi-Square Statistics for all the crosstabs necessary to address the research question: under what circumstances is a Boot Camp Rehabilitation Program Participant likely to recidivate or not after two years (Boot)? Turn in a report which also includes the use of descriptive statistics for the appropriate demographic and substantive variables.

Session V:3
T-Test (Inclass Lab)

During Class complete the necessary, appropriate t-tests for the following in order to give yourself practice and to make sure you've "got it right." Please talk with your professor if you are under about any step. E-mail your findings to the professor, using proper report format--including a table(s).

DeathPen
(1) Research Question 1:
      (a) Do men appear to be more religious then women in this study?
      (b) Are students at Millersville University more religious than those at the University of Wisconsin?

(2) Research Questions 2:
Who is generally most supportive of the death penalty:
      (a) men or women?
      (b) Millersville or Wisconsin students?

Session V:4
T-Test (Homework Lab)

Use proper report format (writing style & tables) to report your research findings in answer to the following research questions.

Boot
Research Questions:
(1) Does being male, completing the program, and/or emerging as a leader in the program appear to reduce one's chances of recidivating (by the end of 2 years after the end of the program)?
(2) Was there a significant increase in re-arrests by the end of 24 months (versus the end of the first 6 months after the program ended)?

Session V:5
ANOVA (Inclass Lab)

During Class complete the necessary, appropriate ANOVA for the following in order to give yourself practice and to make sure you've "got it right." Please talk with your professor if you are unclear about any step. E-mail your findings to the professor, using proper report format--including a table(s).

DeathPen
(1) Research Question 1:
     Does there appear to be a difference in the level of religiosity between those who practice various religions?

(2) Research Questions 2:
     Does there appear to be a difference in level of support for the death penalty between those who practice various religions?

Session V:6
ANOVA (Homework Lab)

Boot

Research Question: Is there a difference in the recidivism after 24 months by educational level?

DeathPen

Research Questions:

(1) Is there a difference in religiosity by political leaning?
(2) Is there a difference in religiosity by economic philosophy?
(3) Is there a difference in support for the death penalty by political leaning?
(4) Is there a difference in support for the death penalty by economic philosophy?

Session V:7
Correlation Coefficient (Inclass Lab)

During class obtain the necessary correlation coefficients in order to answer the research questions noted below. Please talk with your professor if you need any help or advise in completing this lab. Using the proper writing and table format, please e-mail your report in answer to the research questions.

DeathPen

Research Question:
Is one's view on the appropriateness of the death penalty influenced by one's age and/or how religious a person is?

SPSS Sample Data File

Research Question:
What variables contribute to determining how large a salary a worker currently earns (for this training exercise: consider only those variables for which it would be appropriate to compute a correlation coefficient).

Session V:8
Correlation Coefficient (Homework Lab)

Use the proper reporting format (writing style & tables) to report your research findings in answer to the following research question.

Boot
Research Question:
We want to reduce recidivism. What factors have no impact on it, what factors perpetuate recidivism, and what factors make it less likely (for this exercise use variables for which correlation coefficients are appropriate to compute & for recidivism use **recid3**)?

Session V:9
Multiple Regression (Inclass Lab)

SPSS Sample Data File

Build a Multiple Regression Model which best explains why the respondent's current salaries. E-mail the results of the findings section which develops the model.

Session V:10 (Homework Lab)

Boot

Build a Multiple Regression Model which best explains the variables impacting on recidivism (1) within the first 6 months after finishing the rehab program, (2) after the first 12 months, and (3) after 2 years. Explain your findings using a table and proper technical language. Turn in a complete report.

CHAPTER 6

POSTSCRIPT: APPLY IT!

Congratulations, you have made it to the point in the course where you now have the skills to use SPSS to create a data file and to select the statistical tools which are most appropriate for engaging in descriptive and explanatory statistical analysis. These skills will serve you well, not only while you are a student at your current institution, but also in those endeavors you pursue after completing your undergraduate education. Several of my former students have told me they have obtained jobs because of their computer and statistical skills. Several never believed this would occur when they were in my classroom. Some of these students are currently employed in research institutions, several are outdistancing their colleagues in graduate school, while many others are applying their data analysis skills in jobs that would not appear to be a natural venue for such, e.g., probation and parole departments. What about you and your future? I certainly did not anticipate my career path. And for those of you who have been really enjoying this all along, the good news is that you in particular should have a bright future in the information age facilitated by the information highway of the net and the web. There is also much more you can learn beyond this course. See your professor for suggestions. Go for it, it will pay off!

In each of the previous five chapters I showed you what language and writing format to use when reporting your findings using the particular statistical test considered in that chapter section. The purpose of this final chapter is to remind you of what a typical report will contain and to review the statistical tools at your disposal during data analysis.

Report Components. Remember that while this course in data analysis focused on the Findings section of a typical report, there are other sections which the researcher normally must include. A course in Research Methodology normally trains the researcher in how to construct the others. As a reminder (the full discussion was offered in Chapter 1, which you may want to review at this point), let's look at an itemization and summary of all the sections in a report.

> Research Report Title Page
> Abstract
> Statement of the Research Problem or Question(s)
> Literature Review
> Methodology
> Findings
> Conclusions
> Cited References
> Appendices
> > Cited Tables
> > Questionnaire

After the title page, an abstract will summarize what the project addressed, it will identify the source of the data and what statistical procedures were used as well as summarize the key findings. The Statement of the Research Problem and the Literature Review elaborately explain what the focus of the project is, why it is important to obtain an answer to the research question under consideration, and ties what is already known about the issue under investigation to the current study. The Methodology section explains how the data was gathered, what tool was used, from whom the data was gathered, and operationally defines the variables for which data was obtained. The Findings section is the one you are most familiar with as a result of this course. It will usually contain a demographic description of the sample or population under study (although this is also often alternately included in the Methodology section), a description of the substantive variables, and a presentation of the findings pursuant to answering the research question, e.g., chi-square, t-test, correlation coefficients, and/or multiple regression results. The Conclusions section summarizes the findings, notes the limitations of the work, explains the meaning and practical significance of the study, and suggests directions for future work. The References precede the Appendix which is often where we find the tables discussed in the Findings (and sometimes a copy of the data gathering tool, e.g., questionnaire).

Data Analysis Decisions. When approaching data analysis, the researcher must first make sure she is very clear as to which variables are needed to help answer the research question. Looking closely at the codebook, the researcher selects only those which are germane to the issue at hand. The next decision requires her to determine which statistical tests are appropriate for use in this analysis. For example, descriptive statistics are used only when the variable is an interval level variable. Chi-square is selected for only nominal or quasi-nominal variables. T-tests are used when one variable is nominal and the other is interval level. Correlation coefficients and multiple regression are used when each variable is an interval level variable. It is incumbent upon the researcher to use the correct procedure for the variables in the study. Otherwise, the findings will usually be bogus and the conclusions incorrect. A failed effort!

Thank you. I have enjoyed sharing with you how I use SPSS and the most commonly used statistical procedures in sociology. It is my sincere hope that this book assisted you in the process of acquiring these valuable skills. I remember the first time I had to learn how to use a computer to crunch numbers and try to understand how to use and interpret these statistical procedures at the same time. It was difficult for me. I spent many long hours of frustration . . . as well as some joy in the computer center. It was a challenging job, but one which has paid off for your author. If you have tried your best, you should know allot more now than you did when you started this course. Do not lose your skills. Use them or you will lose them. Do a project on your own, do one for another class, do an honors project, do volunteer work that enables you to use these skills (when I was in graduate school I conducted a telephone survey for my brother who was the mayor of Millersville (PA) at that time, I used my newly acquired computer and statistical skills to analyze the data; and to make a long story short, the outcome of that election was altered, at least partly because of what we found and acted upon during the campaign). You may get a job or choose a career in the future that is the result of what you have begun here. Good luck.

Let me know what your computer and statistical future becomes.

Looking at an Example. Now let's return to where we started. Carefully re-read the report used in your class when you started this semester. This report should make much more sense to you now. Identify each section of the report, identify the research question, summarize the findings in answer to this question, and identify which statistics from this course were used in this report.

Applying Your Skills: Complete a Project. Now that you have mastered basic computer skills, the SPSS skills, the basic statistical tools and the basic report writing skills necessary to prepare a report on the findings of your research, it is time to apply these skills. The ultimate test of your mastery, and the ultimate learning experience, is to complete a research project. Your professor will provide you with a list of such projects and one may be assigned to you. Your class might use data from the General Social Survey, the Crime Victimization Studies, or data provided by your professor or this author. A sample list of such projects, based upon data available from your author is included at the end of this chapter. Whichever approach is used in your class, follow your instructor's directions carefully and produce a first rate report. This is the real test of how successful this semester has been. Good luck and enjoy it! This is the "stuff" of what real research is all about. I love it and I believe you will enjoy it too. Yes, I know a grade depends on it, but free yourself to enjoy the quest! Good luck, go to it!!

LAB SESSIONS

Session VI:1
Application Activity: Discerning Types & Uses of Statistics

Let's return to where we began this semester in order to see how far we've come in being able to apply and interpret the statistical procedures we have used this semester. Once again, let's look at the article *The Limited Role of Disaster Experience in Mitigation Adjustment* which was authored by Fischer & Trowbridge. E-mail your answers to the below.

(1) In YOUR OWN WORDS, explain the research question these researchers were trying to address--be specific and accurate (don't just rewrite the article title or you will be wrong!).

(2) Summarize, in your own words, what they found in answer to their research question.

(3) Indicate what types of descriptive statistics they used.

(4) Indicate what types of explanatory statistics they used.

(5) Use Table 3 to write (using proper writing format) your own interpretation of the factors related to how likely the respondents were to believe in the disaster mythology (only write about the TOTAL population, not the individual states).

Session VI:2
End of the Semester Application Lab

Determine what variables you need to examine in order to construct the desired report pursuant to answering the designated research question, determine what descriptive and explanatory statistics you need, obtain the needed output, and begin constructing your report. Use your professor as a research consultant during this process. The report for this lab activity is due by the normal homework due date for your class--please turn in a good "hard copy."

Your report should include a proper title page, an abstract, a good introduction, a complete findings section (demographics, substantives, and statistical examination of pairs of variables to determine if relationships are observed pursuant to answering the research question), a conclusions section (summarizing & interpreting the findings as well as making recommendations--even using sociology to interpret what you found if you can do so), and an appendix for your tables.

I suggest that you organize the third part of your findings section in the following manner for this project: consider pre-bootcamp influences first, then bootcamp influences, and post-boot influences last. Within each of these categories discuss those which do impact (strongest to least) and then those which do not.

WHAT HELPS TO REDUCE RECIDIVISM: WHAT WORKS & WHAT DOES NOT?

Each year federal, state, and local governments spend tax revenues collectively exceeding billions of dollars to combat crime. Sociologists continue to argue that prevention is better then waiting until detention must come into play. They further argue that rehabilitation, i.e., resocialization, is preferable to mere incarceration. Various sociological theories help to explain the circumstances under which human beings deviate and the circumstances under which they may either avoid deviating or cease doing so. For example, we know that differential association helps to either encourage or prevent deviation. We also know that self-attitudes theory also helps to explain how some come to deviate while others do not. Conflict theory, labeling theory, and Merton's Modes of Adaptation are a few of the remaining theories which also help explain deviance versus non-deviance and the circumstances under which one is likely to be able to avoid repeating the deviant behavior.

The current research project draws from data gathered pursuant to evaluating a particular Boot Camp Program designed to rehabilitate juvenile offenders. The goal was to reduce their chance of recidivating. The program director has publicly stated that the Boot Camp Program "is very successful . . . *six months* after completing the program our participants success in avoiding re-arrest demonstrates the appropriateness of the Boot Camp Model for rehabilitation."

As a researcher who has been hired by the state to evaluate this program, share your conclusions about the accuracy of what the program director is saying. Offer some recommendations as to what you, as a program evaluator, would suggest we do pursuant to continuing to monitor and evaluate the degree of success this rehabilitation approach offers.

Session VI:3
Semester Project List (Sample)

Do a thorough job analyzing the data necessary for you to write an excellent report in answer to your assigned research question. Apply *everything* learned this semester.

1. DeathPen.Sav
What factors are associated with one's stand on the death penalty?

2. DeathPen.Sav
What factors are associated with one's degree of religiosity?

3. Alco.Sav
Who was most likely to have ever shop lifted?

4. Alco.Sav
Who was most likely to have made obscene phone calls?

5. Alco.Sav
Who was most likely to have used drugs?

6. Alco.Sav
Who was most likely to have stolen property?

7. Alco.Sav
Who was most likely to have gotten into a fight?

8. Racism.Sav
Who is most likely to have prejudiced attitudes (Prej1)?

9. Racism.Sav
Who is most likely to have prejudiced attitudes (Prej2)?

10. Racism.Sav
Who is most likely to have prejudiced attitudes (Prej3)?

11. Racism.Sav
Who is most likely to have prejudiced attitudes (Prej4)?

12. Boot.Sav
What variables appear to be associated with recidivism 12 months after program completion?

13. Boot.Sav
How did recidivism change between 6 and 12 months after program completion?

14. Boot.Sav
How did recidivism change between 6 and 24 months after program completion?

15. Boot.Sav
How did recidivism change between 12 and 24 months after program completion?

16. SPSS Sample Data
Who is most likely to start out at a high salary?

17. SPSS Sample Data
Who is most likely to end up at a high salary?

18. Your Choice
Examine the codebook of your choice, design your own research question, and do the necessary data analysis to help you report your findings in answer to your research question.

PRESENTATION GUIDELINES

1. Research Report Copies
On Presentation Day the class will be divided into groups of 3 students each. Bring at least 3 copies of your report. Your group members will each need a copy and you will turn one in to me.

2. Analyzing the Reports
On Presentation Day each group member will read and critique the other two reports (see Report Critique Form) before each student takes a turn presenting their findings orally to the group.

3. Oral Presentation & Discussion
On Presentation Day each group member will give a brief oral presentation of their findings in answer to their research question (to last 7-10 minutes). The oral presentations should include at least the following:

Clearly describe the study as it was originally conducted
Clearly explain your research question
Conversationally describe the sample
Conversationally describe the behavior observed (substantive
    frequencies)
Conversationally share what you found re the Research Question
    --make sure in include a statement of what explanatory
    statistics you used & why
Share what you concluded &/or note shortcomings of the original
    study

After each student orally presents, the others are ask any questions they choose to ask the presenter AND they are to share their observations from the critique which note problems or mistakes the researcher made as well as those things the research did very well.

4. To Be Turned In
After the written critiques, oral presentations, and discussions are completed, each group should turn in the following (IN SEPARATE PILES):
Critique Forms
Reports (1 copy from each student)

REPORT CRITIQUE FORM

Your Name: _____

Person Critiqued: _____

Research Question: _____

A. Directions: For each of the following, indicate what was done incorrectly & particularly well

Title Page & Abstract:

Introduction:

Demographics:

Substantive Findings:

Descriptive Statistics:

Explanatory Statistics:

Interpretation of Findings:

Summary/Conclusions:

Tables:

B. Directions: Respond to each of the following
What descriptive statistics were used:
What explanatory statistics were used:
Were the statistics used correctly? Explain.
What would you have done differently?

APPENDIX A

SAMPLE RESEARCH REPORT

THE LIMITED ROLE OF DISASTER EXPERIENCE IN MITIGATION ADJUSTMENT

Continued Subscription to Disaster Mythology Among Local Emergency Management Agency Directors Regardless of Disaster Experience

HENRY W. FISCHER, III

DEPARTMENT OF SOCIOLOGY/ANTHROPOLOGY
MILLERSVILLE UNIVERSITY OF PENNSYLVANIA
MILLERSVILLE, PENNSYLVANIA

1992

A paper presented at the annual meetings of the American Sociological Association in Pittsburgh, Pennsylvania. This research project was supported by a Neimeyer-Hodgson Grant from Millersville University.

ABSTRACT

Ninety-five local emergency managers from two states, Montana and Ohio, responded to a mail-questionnaire which sought to determine if the mitigation adjustment literature is correct is asserting that disaster experience is a poor predictor of mitigation activities. Pearson's correlation coefficients and multiple regression were used to assess the extent to which disaster experience, job experience, and formal education were associated with the degree to which the emergency professionals had developed an accurate perception of the behavioral response problems associated with disasters. The respondents performed poorly on a Likert-scale which measured their belief in the disaster mythology. It is argued that effective mitigation activity would be less likely if the emergency personnel subscribe to the disaster mythology. The findings support the literature in noting that disaster experience is a poor linear predictor. Job experience and professional training experiences were also weak predictors. The most interesting finding was that the younger, better educated emergency personnel seemed to score better than those who had been in the field longer. This finding suggests that mitigation activity, regardless of disaster experience, has the greatest chance of success when the emergency work force consists of professionally trained personnel.

IS IT TRUE THAT DISASTER EXPERIENCE DOES *NOT* RESULT IN MITIGATION ADJUSTMENT?

In 1961 Charles Fritz defined a disaster as an "actual or threatened, accidental, uncontrollable event that is concentrated in time and space, in which a society, or any self-sufficient subdivision of society, undergoes severe danger, and incurs such losses to its members and physical appurtenances that the social structure is disrupted and the fulfillment of all or some of the essential functions of the society are prevented from being completed" (Fischer, 1988a). A natural disaster is one which is caused by the elements of nature, e.g., tornado, earthquake, and hurricane. A technological disaster is one which results from a human-made phenomenon, e.g., air-transportation accident, industrial accident, or conflagration.

If a disaster agent repeatedly strikes a community, does this repeated disaster experience enable the community to become better prepared to defend itself against future such events? In other words, what is the role of disaster experience in mitigation adjustment? If a community is repeatedly struck by severe hurricanes, for example, can we assume that the community's emergency response will become increasingly well-designed to deal with the physical, organizational and behavioral problems commonly found to result from such an event? Or, does disaster experience poorly correlate with mitigation adjustment?

Wenger (1978:41-42) found that one of the primary reasons associated with the formation of a disaster subculture, is the repeated impact of a disaster agent such as a hurricane. The average citizen who survives the repeated impact of a disaster agent appears to often treat future such threats in a cavalier fashion (such as throwing a beer party to watch the hurricane come in). While average citizens may exhibit varied behavioral responses to disaster, what is the pattern observed for professionals, i.e., local emergency officials charged with the responsibility of organizing the community response? Are they likely to learn from their disaster experience? Does their understanding of the physical, organizational and behavioral problems associated with disaster become increasingly accurate with increased disaster experience-- especially if that experience results from the same disaster agent regularly impacting upon their community? While numerous case studies document adoption of mitigative actions by communities after they have experienced a disaster (Drabek, 1986:364-365), the correlation between experience and mitigative actions is not as clear as one might suspect (Rubin, 1981:14-15; Mileti, Drabek, and Haas, 1975:28; Anderson, 1970). For example, there appears to be a short term window of opportunity for the adoption of emerging mitigative change (Drabek, 1986). Mitigation adjustment appears to be more likely to occur where the local government has an affluent tax base, the residents are political activists (and the citizenry is not conservative), the local government exhibits professionalism (and political power is not centralized), and the locale is urbanized (Hutton, Miletti, et al.; 1979). Disaster experience as a predictor of mitigation adjustment appears to be associated, at best, with an, as yet unmapped, decay curve (Drabek, 1986:366). While there is some evidence that disaster events serve to open the constraints that typically restrain the adoption of mitigation adjustments, such effects appear to be temporary-- how temporary is not yet known (Drabek, 1986:366). Most research seeking to understand the circumstances under which mitigative adjustment is likely to occur has been based upon case studies. A fresh methodological approach is urgently needed to facilitate generalization of the findings beyond the community investigated. Several researchers have amassed data which includes hundreds of communities, their findings are, however, still bound by the inherent limitations of field work. Hence, the current study was conceived as one attempt to take an alternative approach to assessing the degree to which disaster experience is not a good predictor of mitigation adjustment.

STUDY'S FOCUS

Disaster researchers have found that average citizens believe in a "disaster mythology." While disaster survivors actually respond in an altruistic manner, the disaster mythology suggests the opposite (Quarantelli and Dynes, 1972; Wenger, et al, 1975; Wenger, et al, 1980; Bryan, 1982; Aga Khan, 1983; Stallings, 1984; Wenger, 1985; Wenger and Friedman, 1986; Johnson, 1987, Quarantelli, 1987; Rubin and Palm, 1987; Johnson, 1987; Fischer, 1988(a), 1988(b) & 1989). The behavioral responses inaccurately believed to occur include: the panic of surviving local citizens, a psychological dependency of the survivors upon emergency personnel, the survivors' inability to function due to their suffering from disaster shock, price gouging by local merchants and/or local citizens, looting by local citizens, and other selfish actions. A declaration of martial law is expected to commonly occur and a total dependence by the stricken community upon outside organizations is seen as normal. It is feared that disaster personnel will desert their posts to assist their own family members rather than serve the community which employs them.

If the repeated impact of a disaster agent assists the community's efforts to better prepare itself for the next such onslaught, then one would expect that such disaster experience would result in emergency personnel gaining an increasingly accurate perception of the physical, organizational, and behavioral problems typically encountered in such a setting. For example, would one not expect that those professionals charged with the responsibility of organizing mitigation adjustment to become less likely to subscribe to the disaster mythology? If disaster experience were correlated with mitigation adjustment, would local emergency managers not become increasingly aware of the fact that looting, price gouging by local merchants, disaster shock, psychological dependency, and so forth, rarely occur? We decided to use belief in the disaster mythology as an indicator of the limited role of disaster experience as a facilitator of mitigation adjustment. We reasoned if disaster response coordinators did not obtain an accurate view of the normal behavioral response to disaster, even after they have gained disaster experience, then their disaster experience is not likely to result in positive mitigation adjustment.

In designing the study, we decided to develop a mail-questionnaire to be completed by the local emergency managers (LEMA's) in two divergent states. We selected a mid-western state, Ohio, and a north-western state, Montana, because of their very different disaster histories and urbanicity. Ohio has not only frequently experienced both technological and natural disasters, but it is home to "tornado alley." Montana was selected because the type of disaster commonly experienced is quite different and the frequency of occurrence is less than the national average. It is also a far less urbanized state than Ohio. The questionnaire was mailed to the emergency manager in each county of the two states (88 counties, hence 88 possible respondents in Ohio and 55 counties, hence 55 possible respondents in Montana). A second mailing was conducted involving those who had not responded to the first one. The response rate was pretty good, 64% (59% for Ohio and 76% for Montana).

Demographic Characteristics (*please refer to Table 1*). The overwhelming majority (81% for the study population, 77% of Montana's lema's and 85% of Ohio's) of the respondents were male, typical of the gender composition of the disaster coordinators nationally. Their average age was 49--the median was 50, (for the total population, 47 for Montana and 51 for Ohio), though the age range was 28 to 77 years of age. The typical lema coordinator completed a few years of college (for total population and for each state), though years of completed formal education ranged from a high school graduate to a holder of a master's degree. More than three-quarters of the respondents (77%) reported completing at least some college, if not an undergraduate degree.

Substantive Variables: Disaster Experience (*please refer to Table 2*). In addition to the usual demographic data, the respondents were asked to indicate how many disaster events they had experienced during their professional life as either a local emergency management (LEMA) coordinator or as an emergency worker below the level of coordinator. Hence, disaster experience was operationalized as the number of disasters in which the respondent had served. The average LEMA coordinator reported responding to four (4) disasters during his career. The number of disasters which the study population reported ranged from zero to thirty-one. Most LEMA coordinators (85%) reported experiencing no more than ten disasters.

Job Experience (*please refer to Table 2*). We also asked the respondent to indicate the level of professional experience and training he or she had, i.e., the number of years served as the LEMA coordinator, the number of years in the field of disaster preparedness, the number of training seminars in which the respondent had participated, and the number of disaster drills in which the respondent had participated. We wanted to assess the extent to which such experiences may have contributed to the disavowal of the disaster mythology. The respondents reported serving an average of seven years in their position as LEMA coordinator and thirteen years working within the disaster field. Job experience ranged from a few months to forty years as a LEMA coordinator and to forty-two years within the field generally. The average number of training seminars reportedly attended by the LEMA coordinators was thirteen. Slightly more than half (55%) of the respondents reported attending not more than ten seminars. Lema coordinators averaged participating in ten disaster drills during their career. A majority reported participating in less than ten, a few respondents reported participation in a large number of drills which skewed the average-- one respondent reported participating in 100 such drills.

Belief in Disaster Mythology (*please refer to Table 2* & Appendix Item A). And finally, the respondent was also asked to respond to a series of Likert scaled statements regarding aspects of the disaster mythology, e.g., he was asked to indicate the extent to which he perceived that looting on the part of local citizens would be a problem needing his attention after a disaster impacts his community. The respondent was asked to indicate the likelihood of each of twenty items being problematic during a disaster event. He was asked to scale his response as "very likely," "likely," "unlikely," or "very unlikely." We then coded the respondent's answer as "0" if he rated a myth from the disaster mythology as very likely or likely to occur or as "1" if he rated a myth as not (very) likely to occur. Conversely, we coded the respondent's answer as "1" if he rated an accurate statement as very likely or likely to occur or as "0" if he rated an accurate statement as (very) unlikely to occur. The summed scaled responses could range from a low score of zero (meaning he completely believes in the disaster myths) to a maximum of twenty (which suggests that he has a completely accurate perception of the behavioral response in a disaster). In this study, the scores ranged five to eighteen. The mean score was thirteen (for the study population as well as for both the Montana and Ohio LEMA coordinators). If a student were to score a thirteen out of twenty on a quiz, the accompanying grade would be a "D" (65%)! We were shocked that the paid professionals would score so poorly. This is particularly worrisome considering the vast job experience reported above.

LITERATURE SUPPORTED: EXPERIENCE IS *NOT* A GOOD LINEAR PREDICTOR

We next sought to determine the extent to which disaster experience correlated with the LEMA coordinator's belief in the disaster mythology. As noted above, case studies of various impacted communities have found that disaster experience alone is not a good predictor of long-term mitigation adjustment. The present study sought to assess this finding through a methodological approach that is designed to facilitate the ability to generalize whatever is found beyond the individual cases studied through field work. We decided to also assess the degree to which disaster training and the selected demographic variables appear to either facilitate or mitigate against belief in the disaster mythology.

Disaster Experience: A Weak Predictor (*please refer to Table 3 & Plot 1*). A Pearson's Correlation Coefficient was computed to assess the influence of disaster experience (operationalized as the number of disasters the respondent experienced during his career) on the LEMA coordinator's belief in the disaster mythology. A weak direct relationship was observed (r = .159*; a population was studied, not a sample, the probability level is moot), suggesting that either the number of disasters to which the LEMA coordinator responded during his career has minimal influence on improving the accuracy of his perception of the behavioral response problems commonly encountered during a disaster, or the relationship that does exist is not linear. We examined a scatterplot in an attempt to determine if the latter is true. The results suggest that there may be some linearity to the weak relationship. Alternately the argument could certainly be made that a threshold exists beyond which experience does result in the rejection of the disaster mythology. The reader will note how the limited disaster experience of a LEMA director appears to have no relationship to myth subscription or disavowal (see the diffuse scattered pattern), while greater experience begins to result in a higher accuracy score which does appear to be linear in nature.

Job Experiences: Weak Predictors (*please refer to Table 3*). Pearson's Correlation Coefficients were also computed to determine if the LEMA coordinator was more likely accurately perceive the post-disaster behavioral response problems if he had extensive job experience (measured in two ways: years a LEMA coordinator and total number of years worked in the disaster field). We also examined the influence of training experiences, i.e., the number of disaster response training seminars and disaster drills in which the LEMA coordinator participated. The findings suggest that a weak relationship exists for each, but the relationship between mythology subscription and the total number of years worked in the field is of particular interest. A weak direct relationship was observed for the number of years the LEMA coordinator has served in this position (r = .159), the number of training seminars in which the coordinator has participated (r = .135), and the number of disaster drills in which the coordinator has participated (r = .100). Hence, we conclude that such job experiences do somewhat increase the likelihood that the LEMA coordinator will gain an increasingly accurate perspective on the behavioral response problems that occur as a result of the impact of a disaster agent upon his community; however, such work experiences do not appear to make it far more likely that this will be the outcome. And, if their perceptions of the behavioral response problems are not affected by work experience, given the low average mythology score found in this study, can we not, at least tentatively, assume that effective mitigation adjustment is doomed? Why both disaster and job experience fail influence the coordinator's perception of the problems he will encounter in future disasters will be explored in the concluding section of this paper.

It is particularly interesting to note that the final indicator of job experience, the total number of years in which the LEMA coordinator has worked within the disaster field, was found to be inversely correlated with belief in the disaster mythology. A weak, inverse relationship (r = -.108) was observed which suggests that those new to the field, for whatever reason(s), may be more likely to reject the mythology than their counterparts who have worked in the field for many years. Why might this be the case? Quite possibly, the newer coordinators, as part of a younger generation, may be better educated, which may result in a more accurate perception of behavioral response in a disaster.

Education & Age (*please refer to Table 3*). To investigate this hypothesis, we computed Pearson Correlation Coefficients for the number of years of formal education completed by the LEMA coordinators and their current age in years with their mythology score. We found a weak, inverse relationship (r = -.112) for age and a stronger (the strongest correlation observed in the study), direct relationship for education (r = .239; for Montana the correlation is even stronger, r = .403). These findings support our hypothesis that perhaps the newer, i.e., younger, LEMA coordinators are more likely to reject the disaster mythology as a result of being better educated generally. If this is true, and please note we are *only* hypothesizing at this juncture, then there may be some hope for the future as a generation subscription scores among the LEMA coordinators than those studied of professional LEMA coordinators come into office. Both the researchers and the reader must remember, however, that the correlation coefficients are not very strong, suggesting that other

---

*For purposes of interpretation in this study, we defined an r = .000 to .200 as a "weak" relationship; an r = .201 to .400 as a "somewhat weak" relationship; a r = .401 to .600 as a "somewhat strong" relationship; an r = .601 to .800 as a "strong" relationship; and an r = .801 to 1.000 as a "very strong relationship.

unidentified variables may explain more of the variation in mythology presently. Future research will have to address this issue.

Multiple Regression Assessment (*please refer to Table 4*). To further assess the relative influence of each of the substantive and relevant demographic variables' influence on mythology subscription scores of the LEMA coordinators, we computed a step-wise multiple regression model which contained the fewest number of variables that explained the most variation. We found that the beta values for the number of years the respondent has worked in the disaster field (-.327), the number of years the respondent has spent serving as a LEMA coordinator (.181), the number of years of formal education the respondent has completed (.175), the number of disasters experienced by the coordinator (.151), and the number of training seminars in which the coordinator has participated (.148) combine to explain approximately 15% (R squared = .151, Multiple R = .389) of the variation in the mythology subscription scores. The strength and inverse nature of the relative relationship between years of work experience in the disaster field and the mythology score suggest, again, that the newer coordinators may be less likely to believe in the mythology. And, since the beta value for educational experience is higher than that for disaster experience, training seminars, and drills, we suggest that the data, at least tentatively, support the argument that a younger professionalized work force is more likely to accurately perceive the behavioral response problems associated with a disaster. Hence, this professionalized work force would quite possibly be better able to work for effective mitigation adjustment whether they awaited the impact of a disaster upon their community or not. They may be better positioned to work for mitigation before or after the impact time period. This argument is not inconsistent with the disaster research literature generally. We must note, however, that this same literature does suggest that other variables do play a role in determining when and if mitigation activities during any time period are effectively adopted. In our view, further mapping of the parameters of such are necessary at this juncture of the literature's development.

SUMMARY

The objective of the current study was to assess the literature's contention that disaster experience does not, in itself, lead to disaster mitigation adjustment. Most of this literature has been developed through numerous case studies of communities which were recovering from a disaster. We sought to circumvent the inherent limitations on the ability to generalize from field work, by surveying two populations of local emergency management coordinators. What we found was both discomforting, yet hopeful. The professional emergency responders averaged 65% (a grade equivalent to a "D") on the "test" of their knowledge of the disaster mythology. We argue that a LEMA coordinator who incorrectly perceives the common behavioral response problems associated with a disaster event is unlikely to effectively develop mitigation activities which will result in being better prepared for the next impact. We are hopeful, however, about the future. We found that there may be a tendency for a newer, younger, better educated, professional work force of LEMA coordinators to accurately perceive the behavioral response problems associated with a disaster. It is our hope that mitigation adjustment will be facilitated as a result.

We wondered why, however, disaster experience alone would not translate into a higher, more accurate perception of behavioral response problems in the present study. Quarantelli (1988) has perhaps already provided that answer, when he wrote of the tendency for emergency planners to work from a "command-and-control" model. Drawing from Quarantelli, we would argue that the tendency for LEMA coordinators to perceive their task as that of managing the community response, rather than engaging in mitigation activities and leading the community members in planning their own response. In turn, this is likely to lead to the LEMA coordinator's viewing his role as working from the EOC to manage the organizational response while being effectively cut off from knowing the actual behavioral response in the field. He is then reduced to hearing from others what either may be accurate portrayals of the problems or rumor. Whichever it is, it tends to be disseminated to the general population through the mass media when he holds a press conference, resulting in further reinforcement for and belief in the disaster mythology if it is rumor that he receives (Fischer, 1989).

Caveats. The methodological approach of the current study was deliberately selected in order to circumvent the limitations of field work, the most frequently utilized method in disaster research generally. The mail-questionnaire, of course, has it's own limitations. The problems related to the "self-report" nature of such survey research has been documented frequently by Babbie (1992) and others. We wondered, for example, about the accuracy of the self-reporting of the participation in "100 disaster drills." We were also uncomfortable with the reporting of the number of disasters in which the LEMA coordinator allegedly participated. It was clear that several respondents were estimating their experience and other respondents included severe snow storms as disasters. We doubted the efficacy of those storms meeting Fritz's definition of disaster. They may, but the point we wish to make is that the methodology employed herein did not clarify to our satisfaction the difference between emergencies and disasters, resulting, in our belief, in inaccuracies in the reporting of disaster experience. An attempt to reduce the extent of such error in the future might include providing the respondent with a clear distinction between the two before asking him to self-report disaster experience. Of course, it would be preferable to obtain some behavioral indicator if that were feasible. And finally, the response rate was good, but survey researchers always seek a return rate of 100%. A follow-up phone call prior to doing a third mailing may assist in attaining a result that is closer to the ideal.

Future Endeavors. The numerous case studies developed through meticulous field work have made, and will continue to make, great contributions to the literature. We need to continue to investigate the answers to the various research questions posed by the literature through methodologies, however, that will facilitate generalization beyond the individual cases studied. Hence, we would like to see disaster researchers continue to develop survey research projects that will assess the activities of the populations of research interest. The current project should be viewed as a limited pilot study. Beyond disaster experience, job experience, and completed education, there are many variables that need to be investigated pursuant to mapping the circumstances under which mitigation adjustment occurs. The short term window of opportunity for the adoption of emerging mitigative actions and the accompanying decay curve that Drabek notes (1986) needs further investigation. The noted effect on mitigative actions of an affluent tax base, of local political activism, of a non-centralized local government, and urbanization (Hutton, Miletti, et al.; 1979) must be further mapped. The current findings are one contribution to this continuing effort.

REFERENCES

Aga Khan, Prince Sadruddin. 1983 (Nov/Dec). "Disasters: Myth and Reality." Undro News.

Anderson, William A. "Tsunami Warnings in Crescent City, California and Hilo, Hawaii." Pp. 116-124 in The Great Alaska Earthquake of 1964: Human Ecology, Committee on the Alaska Earthquake of the National Research Council (ed.). Washington, D.C.: National Academy of Sciences.

Babbie, Earl. 1992. The Practice of Social Research. Belmont, California: Wadsworth Publishing Company.

Bryan, John L. 1982 (March). "Human Behavior in the MGM Grand Hotel Fire." Fire Journal: Vol. 76 No. 2.

Collier, James. 1962 (February). "How Would You Act in a Disaster?" Pageant.

Drabek, Thomas E. 1986. Human System Responses to Disaster: An Inventory of Sociological Findings. New York: Springer-Verlag.

Fischer, Henry W., III. 1988(a). "Behavioral and Organizational Response to Disaster." Alliance, Ohio: Social Research Center, Mount Union College.

Fischer, Henry W., III. 1988(b). "Disastrous Fantasizing in the Print Media: Differences in How Natural Versus Technological Disasters Are Portrayed Over a Forty Year Period." Alliance, Ohio: Social Research Center, Mount Union College.

Fischer, Henry W., III. 1989. "Hurricane Gilbert: The Media's Creation of the Storm of the Century During September 1988." Boulder, Colorado: The Natural Research and Applications Center, The University of Colorado.

Hutton, Janice R., Dennis S. Mileti, with William B. Lord, John H. Sorensen, and Marvin Waterstone. 1979. "Analysis of Adoption and Implementation of Community Land Use Regulations for Floodplains." San Francisco: Woodward-Clyde Consultants.

Johnson, Norris. 1987 (August). "Panic and the Breakdown of Social Order: Popular Myth, Social Theory, Empirical Evidence." Sociological Focus. Vol. 20 No. 3.

Keating, John P. 1982 (May). "The Myth of Panic." Fire Journal.

Mileti, Dennis S., Thomas E. Drabek, and J. Eugene Haas. 1975. Human Systems in Extreme Environments. Boulder, Colorado: Institute of Behavioral Science, The University of Colorado.

Perrow, Charles. 1984. Normal Accidents: Living with High Risk Technologies. New York: Basic Books.

Perry, Joseph B., Jr., Randolph Hawkins, and David M. Neal. 1983. "Giving and Receiving Aid." International Journal of Mass Emergencies and Disasters 1 (March):171-188.

Perry, Ronald W. 1985. Comprehensive emergency Management: Evacuating Threatened Populations. Greenwich, Connecticut, and London: JAI Press, Inc.

Perry, Ronald W., David F. Gillespie, and Dennis S. Mileti. 1974. "System Stress and the Persistence of Emergent Organizations." Sociological Inquiry 44 (No. 2):111-119.

Quarantelli, E.L. 1982 (Nov/Dec). "Reality and Myth in Community Disasters." Undro News.

Quarantelli, E.L. 1987. "Researching and Managing Human Behavior in Disasters." Newark, Delaware: Disaster Research Center, The University of Delaware.

Quarantelli, E.L. 1987. "The Social Science Study of Disasters and Mass Communications." Newark, Delaware: Disaster Research Center, The University of Delaware.

Quarantelli, E.L. 1988. "Local Emergency Management Agencies: Research Findings On Their Progress and Problems in the Last Two Decades." Newark, Delaware: Disaster Research Center, The University of Delaware.

Quarantelli, E.L. and Dynes, Russel R. 1972. "Images of Disaster Behavior: Myths and Consequences." Newark, Delaware: Disaster Research Center, The University of Delaware.

Rossi, Peter H., James D. Wright, Sonia R. Wright, and Eleanor Weber-Burdin. 1978. "Are There Long Term Effects of American Natural Disasters?" Mass Emergencies 3:117-132.

Rubin, Claire. 1981. "Long-Term Recovery from Natural Disasters: A Comparative Analysis of Six Local Experiences." Washington, D.C.: The Academy for Contemporary Problems, The Resource Referral Service.

Rubin, Claire B. and Palm, Risa. 1987. "National Origin and Earthquake Response: Lessons from the Whittier Narrow Earthquake of 1987." International Journal of Mass Emergencies and Disasters. Vol. 53, pp. 347-356.

Scanlon, T. Joseph, and Suzanne Alldred 1982. "Media Coverage of Disasters: The Same Old Story." Emergency Planning Digest 9 (October-December):13-19.

Scanlon, T. Joseph with Kim Dixon and Scott McClellan. 1982. "The Miramichi Earthquakes: The Media Respond to an Invisible Emergency." Ottawa, Ontario, Canada: Emergency Communications Research Unit, School of Journalism, Carleton University.

Wenger, Dennis E., et al. 1975. "It's a Matter of Myth: An Empirical Examination of Individual Insights into Disaster Research." Disasters and Mass Media. Washington, D.C.: The National Academy of Sciences.

Wenger, Dennis E. 1978. "Community Response to Disaster: Functional and Structural Alterations." Pp. 17-47 in Disasters: Theory and Research, E.L. Quarantelli (ed.). Beverly Hills, California: Sage.

Wenger, Dennis. 1980. "Some Observations on the Nature of Panic Behavior A Normative Orientation." Newark, Delaware: Disaster Research Center, The University of Delaware.

Wenger, Dennis E. 1985. "Mass Media and Disaster." Newark, Delaware: Disaster Research Center, The University of Delaware.

Wenger, Dennis E., and Friedman, Barbara. 1986. "Local and National Media Coverage of Disasters: A Content Analysis of the Print Media's Treatment of Disaster Myths." Newark, Delaware: Disaster Research Center, The University of Delaware.

Wenger, Dennis E., Thomas F. James, and Charles F. Faupel. 1980. "Disaster Beliefs and Emergency Planning." Newark, Delaware: Disaster Research Project, University of Delaware.

TABLE 1: SELECTED DEMOGRAPHIC CHARACTERISTICS

		Total Population N = 95	Montana N = 43	Ohio N=52
Gender	Male	81%	77%	85%
	Female	19%	23%	15%
		100%	100%	100%
Age	$\leq$ 50	55%	60%	48%
	> 50	45%	40%	52%
		100%	100%	100%
Education				
High School		23%	16%	27%
Some College +		77%	84%	73%
		100%	100%	100%

TABLE 2:   DISASTER EXPERIENCE, JOB EXPERIENCE, & MYTHOLOGY BELIEF

	Total Population N = 95	Montana N = 43	Ohio N=52
Disaster Experience			
≤ 10 Disasters	85%	83%	85%
> 10 Disasters	15%	17%	15%
	100%	100%	100%
Years As LEMA Coordinator			
≤ 10 Years	77%	67%	77%
> 10 Years	23%	33%	23%
	100%	100%	100%
Years in Emergency Field			
≤ 10 Years	53%	56%	52%
> 10 Years	47%	56%	48%
	100%	100%	100%
Disaster Seminars			
≤ 10 Seminars	55%	46%	55%
> 10 Seminars	45%	54%	45%
	100%	100%	100%
Disaster Drills			
≤ 10 Drills	68%	66%	70%
> 10 Drills	32%	34%	30%
	100%	100%	100%
Mythology Belief Score			
≤ 13 Accurate Items	41%	35%	46%
> 13 Accurate Items	59%	65%	54%
	100%	100%	100%

TABLE 3: PEARSON'S CORRELATION COEFFICIENTS FOR RELATIONSHIPS BETWEEN DISASTER MYTHOLOGY SCORE & SELECTED VARIABLES
N = 95

	# Disasters Experienced	Yrs LEMA Director	Yrs Work Field	Seminars	Drills	Educ	Age
Myth Scores:							
Pop .159	.143	-.108	.135	.100	.239	-.112	
Mont .126	.128	-.019	.207	.174	.403	.098	
Ohio .153	.135	-.146	.098	.069	.055	-.057	

[Please note: data gathered on a population, not a sample; it is therefore inappropriate to compute probability levels]

TABLE 4:   MULTIPLE REGRESSION FOR DISASTER MYTHOLOGY SCORE & SELECTED VARIABLES
N = 95

Variable	B	SE B	Beta	T	Sig T
# Disasters	.062	.044	.151	1.406	.163
Education	.340	.202	.175	1.683	.096
Seminars	.025	.021	.148	1.178	.242
Yrs Field	-.076	.030	-.327	-2.496	.015
Yrs LEMA Dir	.067	.052	.181	1.302	.197
(Constant)	11.52827	.810		14.226	.000

Multiple R = .3837   R Square = .147   Standard Error = 2.39

	DF	Sum of Squares	Mean Square
Regression	5	84.963	16.993
Residual	86	492.200	5.723

F = 2.97   Significance of F = .016

[Please note: data gathered on a population, not a sample; probability levels moot]

DISASTER MYTHOLOGY SCORING FORM

Please indicate the degree to which you believe each of the below will be a problem that will require an organized emergency management response (by your office, and/or police, fire, etc.) in the event that a disaster strikes your community.

Please use the following rating scale:

(1) very unlikely to occur
(2) unlikely to occur
(3) likely to occur
(4) very likely to occur)

SCORED:

(a) individual citizens panic — "1" answer 1 or 2, "0" answer 3 or 4
(b) panic by local leaders — "1" answer 1 or 2, "0" answer 3 or 4
(c) looting by residents of the community — "1" answer 1 or 2, "0" answer 3 or 4
(d) looting by non-locals — "0" answer 1 or 2, "1" answer 3 or 4
(e) price gouging by local merchants — "1" answer 1 or 2, "0" answer 3 or 4
(f) price gouging by local private citizens — "1" answer 1 or 2, "0" answer 3 or 4
(g) price gouging by people coming into town — "0" answer 1 or 2, "1" answer 3 or 4
(h) local residents refuse to evacuate — "0" answer 1 or 2, "1" answer 3 or 4
(i) local residents behave irrationally — "1" answer 1 or 2, "0" answer 3 or 4
(j) local residents go site seeing — "0" answer 1 or 2, "1" answer 3 or 4
(k) local residents will not prepare — "1" answer 1 or 2, "0" answer 3 or 4
(l) local residents will not help — "1" answer 1 or 2, "0" answer 3 or 4
(m) outsiders will converge — "0" answer 1 or 2, "1" answer 3 or 4
(n) search depends on outsiders — "1" answer 1 or 2, "0" answer 3 or 4
(o) survivors will not know what to do — "1" answer 1 or 2, "0" answer 3 or 4
(p) survivors will behave very selfishly — "1" answer 1 or 2, "0" answer 3 or 4
(q) emergency workers will be selfish — "1" answer 1 or 2, "0" answer 3 or 4
(r) emergency workers will leave posts — "1" answer 1 or 2, "0" answer 3 or 4
(s) evacuees go to homes of relatives — "0" answer 1 or 2, "1" answer 3 or 4
(t) more clothing than needed donated — "0" answer 1 or 2, "1" answer 3 or 4

A SCORE OF "1" WAS GIVEN WHEN THE ANSWER GIVEN IS NORMALLY TRUE OR PROBABLE, AS FOUND IN THE RESEARCH LITERATURE.

A SCORE OF "0" WAS GIVEN WHEN THE ANSWER GIVE IS NORMALLY PART OF THE DISASTER MYTHOLOGY, AS FOUND IN THE RESEARCH LITERATURE.

APPENDIX B

CODEBOOKS

JUVENILE BOOTCAMP REHAB ASSESSMENT
Codebook: BOOT.SAV

[1] SEX   Gender of Rehab Bootcamp Participant
                            1   Female
                            2   Male

[2] COMPLETE   Did Participant Complete Entire 26 Weeks of
                            the Bootcamp Program (versus drop out/get
                            thrown out of Program)?
                            1   Yes
                            2   No

[3] LEADER   Did Participant Emerge as a Leader During the
                            Bootcamp Program?
                            1   Yes
                            2   No

[4] RECID1 Number of Times Participant Was Arrested Again
                            Within 6 Months of Completing the Program?
                            [Actual Number of Times]

[5] RECID2 Number of Times Participant Was Arrested Again
                            Within 12 Months of Completing the Program?
                            [Actual Number of Times]

[6] RECID3 Number of Times Participant Was Arrested Again
                            Within 24 Months of Completing the Program?
                            [Actual Number of Times]

[7] GANG   Belong to a Gang Before Joing Program?
                            1   Yes
                            2   No

[8] Return Return to old neighborhood after completing Program?
                            1   Yes
                            2   No

[9] Father   Number of Times Father was ever arrested?
                            [Actual Number of Times]

[10] Mother Number of Times Mother was ever arrested?
                            [Actual Number of Times]

[11] SIBS   Number of Times any & all siblings were ever arrested?
[Actual Number of Times]

[12] Friends Number of Times best friends were ever arrested?
[Actual Number of Times]

[13] EDUC Formal Education Completed to date:
            1   Less than high school
            2   High School grad
            3   Some College Completed
            4   College Grad
            5   Graduate School Begun
            6   Competed Graduate Degree(s)--
e.g., M.A., Ph.D.

CAPITAL PUNISHMENT SURVEY
Codebook: DEATHPEN.SAV

1. SEX   1 Male
               2 Female

2. AGE   [actual number of years]

3. RACE
          1 Afro-American   4 Asian
          2 Caucasian   5 Other
          3 Hispanic

4. SCHOOL
          1 Millersville
          2 UW - Stevens Point

5. RELIGION
          1 Catholic   3 Protestant
          2 Jewish   4 None (Agnostic or Atheist)
                      5 Other

6. Politic   Political leaning for social issues
          1 Conservative
          2 Moderate
          3 Liberal

7. Economic Political leaning for economic issues
          1 Conservative
          2 Moderate
          3 Liberal

8. Class   Ever taken class dealing with death penalty?
          1 Yes
          2 No

PLEASE NOTE:
THE ANSWERS TO QUESTIONS 9-18 ARE CODED AS
FOLLOWS TO CREATE THE MEASURE "RELSCORE"
(a measure of how religious a person is):

1. Never	=	0
2. Rarely	=	1
3. Occasionally	=	2
4. Often	=	3
5. Always/Very often	=	4

HOW OFTEN DO YOU DO EACH OF THE FOLLOWING:

9. ATTEND	attend services?
10. PRAY	pray or meditate?
11. SUNSCHOO	attend Sunday school?
12. USHER	usher or help out?
13. COMMITTE	participate in church committees?
14. CHARITY	participate in charity or missions work?
15. DONATE	make donations to your church?
16. CHOIR	participate in the choir?
17. CAMPUS	participate in campus religious groups?
18. SOCIALS	attend church social functions?

PLEASE NOTE THAT THE ANSWERS TO QUESTIONS 19-30 ARE CODED AS FOLLOWS TO CREATE THE MEASURE "BELIEF" (a measure of how strongly the person favors the death penalty):

> 1 Support (1)
> 2 Oppose (0)

DO YOU FAVOR OR OPPOSE THE DEATH PENALTY FOR EACH OF THE FOLLOWING?

19. RAPE	Persons convicted of rape?
20. REPEAT	Repeat offenders of three or more violent crimes?
21. POLICE	Convicted of murdering policemen, prison guards, or judges?
22. SERIAL	Convicted of several carefully planned murders?
23. DRUALCO	Convicted of murdering while under the influence?
24. GANG	Murders as a result of a gang-related incident?
25. ARGUMENT	Murder in the "heat of an argument" against a family member or acquaintence?
26. MENTAL	Murderers who are medically diagnosed mentally ill?
27. JUVENILE	Murder while under the age of 18?
28. HIRE	People who hire someone else to commit a murder?
29. VICTIM	Person killed one of your family members or friends?
30. FAMCRIM	Murderer was one of your family members or friends?

31. BELIEF   Computed measure for how strongly respondent
                    favors capital punishment (possible range of
                    scores is from 0 - 12, 0 represents totally against
                    capital punishment under any circumstances
                    while 12 represents favoring capital punishment
                    under all circumstances)

                    [actual number, 0 - 12]

32. RELSCORE   Computed measure for how religious respondent
                    is (possible range of scores is from 0 - 40, 0
                    represents not religious at all while 40 represents
                    extremely religious)

                    [actual number, 0 - 40]

ALCOHOL STUDY
Codebook: ALCO.SAV

1. SEX

Male	= 1
Female	= 2

2. AGE   Actual number given

3. RACE

Caucasian	= 1
Afro-American	= 2
Hispanic	= 3
Asian	= 4
Other	= 5

4. CLASS   (Class Standing)

Freshman	= 1
Sophomore	= 2
Junior	= 3
Senior	= 4
Graduate	= 5

5. GPA   (Grade point average)

3.50 - 4.00	= 1
3.00 - 3.49	= 2
2.50 - 2.99	= 3
2.00 - 2.49	= 4
1.50 - 1.99	= 5
1.00 - 1.49	= 6
Below 1.00	= 7

6. RESIDENCE (Where do you live?)

Dormitory	= 1
Apart./House	= 2
Parent's Home	= 3
Other	= 4

7. DRINK

(Do you drink alcoholic beverages?)
Yes   = 1
No   = 2

8. OFTEN

(How often do you drink?)
Once a month   = 1
Two per month = 2
2-3 times a week= 3
4-5 times a week= 4
5+ per week   = 5

9. TYPE

(What type of alcohol do you usually drink?)
Beer   = 1
Wine   = 2
Liquor   = 3

10. Amount

(How much do you usually consume at one sitting?)
1 drink   = 1
2-3 drinks   = 2
4-5 drinks   = 3
6-9 drinks   = 4
10 or more   = 5

11. OBSCENE

(Have you ever make obscene phone calls?)
Yes   = 1
No   = 2

12. FIGHT

(Have you ever been in a physical fight?)
Yes   = 1
No   = 2

13. DESTROY

(Have you ever destroyed/defaced public/private property?)
Yes   = 1
No   = 2

14. STOLENSS

(Have you ever stolen street signs?)
Yes   = 1
No   = 2

15. STOLENPP   (Have you ever stolen someone's personal
                  property?)
                  Yes   = 1
                  No   = 2

16. SHOPLIFT   (Have you ever shoplifted from a store?)
                  Yes   = 1
                  No   = 2

17. DUI   (Have you ever driven while under the influence
                  of alcohol?)
                  Yes   = 1
                  No   = 2

18. DRUGS   (Have you ever used illegal drugs?)
                  Yes   = 1
                  No   = 2

RACISM STUDY
Codebook: RACISM.SAV

1. SEX

Male	=	1
Female	=	2

2. AGE   Actual number given

3. RACE

Caucasian	=	1
African American	=	2
Asian	=	3
Latino	=	4
Other	=	5

4. CLASS

Freshman	=	1
Sophomore	=	2
Junior	=	3
Senior	=	4
Graduate	=	5

5. POLAFFIL

Republican	=	1
Democrat	=	2
Independent	=	3
Other	=	4

6. RESIDENC   (Where do you permanently reside?)

Large City	=	1
Small City	=	2
Suburbs	=	3
Rural Area	=	4

7. NEIGHBOR   (Does your neighborhood primarily consist of
                     people from:)
                     Same Race   = 1
                     Various Races   = 2
                     Different Race   = 3

8. HISCHOOL   (What was the racial distribution of your HS?)
                     All Caucasian   = 1
                     Integrated but mostly caucasian   = 2
                     All African American   = 3
                     Integrated but mostly African American   = 4
                     Other   = 5

9. FRIENDS   Actual percentage of friends from a different
                     race or ethnic background.

10. YOURVIEW   Actual scaled number from 1-5.

11. PARVIEW   Actual scaled number from 1-5.

PLEASE NOTE: FOR QUESTIONS 12-15 THE ANSWERS ARE
SCORED AS FOLLOWS

Strongly Agree   = 1
Agree   = 2
Neutral   = 3
Disagree   = 4
Strong Disagree = 5

12. ASSOCIAT   ("I like to associate with people from
                races/cultures other than my own.")

13. EQTREAT   ("All people should be treated equally by the
                police and the courts.")

14. SOCCLUB   ("A social club that excludes due to ethnic/racial
                background is morally unacceptable.")
15. MARRIAGE   ("I accept interracial marriages.")

16. PREJ1   Actual sum of answers to questions numbered
                12-15 (range from 4 to 20, 4 no prejudice while
                20 represents high prejudice).

PLEASE NOTE: FOR QUESTIONS 17-22 THE ANSWERS ARE
SCORED AS FOLLOWS

Yes = 1
No   = 0

17. SUPERSTI   (Is there a difference in levels of superstition according to race?)

18. AMBITION   (Is there a difference in amounts of ambition according to race?)

19. EDUC   (Is there a difference in the valuing of a good education according to race?)

20. ACADABIL   (Is there a difference in academic ability according to race?)

21. INTELL   (Is there a difference in levels of intelligence according to race?)

22. TRUST   (Is there a difference in how trustworthy one is according to race?)

23. PREJ2   Actual sum of answers to questions numbered 17-22 (range from 0 to 6, 0 no prejudice while 6 represents high prejudice).

PLEASE NOTE: FOR QUESTIONS 24-27 THE ANSWERS ARE
SCORED AS FOLLOWS

Very Concerned	=	1
Somewhat Concerned	=	2
Neutral	=	3
Not Concerned	=	4

24. RELATION   (How concerned are you about racial relations
in general?)

25. PREJUDIC   (How concerned are you about racial
prejudice?)

26. OPPORTUN   (How concerned are you about inequality of
opportunity in America?)

27. HATECRIM   (How concerned are you about the number of
hate crimes in the United States?)

28. PREJ3   Actual sum of answers to questions numbered
24-27 (range from 4 to 16, 4 no prejudice while
16 represents high prejudice).

PLEASE NOTE: FOR QUESTIONS 29-32 THE ANSWERS ARE
SCORED AS FOLLOWS

Yes = 1
No = 0

29. DISCRIM   (Do you think that minority groups have worse
jobs, income, and housing than caucasians due
to discrimination?)

30. EDUC   (Do you think minority groups have worse jobs,
income, and housing than caucasians because
they do not have the education it takes to rise
out of poverty?)

31. NOMOTIV   (Do you think minority groups have worse jobs,
income, and education than caucasians because
they do not have the motivation or will power
to pull themselves out of poverty?)

32. NOINTEL   (Do you think that minority groups have worse
jobs, incomes, and housing because they do not
have the intelligence it takes to rise out of
poverty?)

33. PREJ4   Actual sum of answers to questions numbered
29-32 (range from 0 to 4, 0 no prejudice while
4 represents high prejudice).

34. COURSES   (What courses have you taken or are currently
registered for?)
American History   = 1
Afro-American History   = 2
Modern Jewish History   = 3
Inter-American Relations   = 4
Race & Ethnic Relations   = 5
Human Relations   = 6
Oriental Philosophy   = 7
Psychology of Racism   = 8

SPSS SAMPLE DATA
Codebook

1. ID   Identification Code (not an actual variable, just code to identify respondent)

2. SALBEG   Beginning Salary [actual dollars]

3. SEX   Gender

Male	=	0
Female	=	1

4. TIME   Job Seniority [time on job given in months]

5. AGE   Age [years given]

6. SALNOW   Salary Paid now [in dollars]

7. EDLEVEL   Years of formal education completed

8. WORK   Work Experience

9. JOBCAT   Employment category code (not useful as a variable)

10. MINORITY   Minority or not?

white	=	0
nonwhite	=	1

11. SEXRACE   Sex and Race Combinations of Respondent

White Male	=	1
White Female	=	2
Black Male	=	3
Black Female	=	4

APPENDIX C

RAW DATA

JUVENILE BOOTCAMP REHAB ASSESSMENT
Codebook: BOOT.SAV

The variables are listed in the following order:
LINE   1: COMPLETE EDUC FATHER FRIENDS GANG LEADER MOTHER
LINE   2: RECID1 RECID2 RECID3 RETURN SEX SIBS

COMPLETE:	1.00	1.00	5.00	18.00	1.00	2.00	.00
RECID1:	1.00	3.00	7.00	1.00	2.00	6.00	
COMPLETE:	1.00	1.00	8.00	42.00	1.00	2.00	.00
RECID1:	2.00	6.00	13.00	1.00	2.00	25.00	
COMPLETE:	1.00	1.00	9.00	49.00	1.00	2.00	.00
RECID1:	3.00	7.00	15.00	1.00	2.00	27.00	
COMPLETE:	1.00	1.00	10.00	53.00	1.00	2.00	1.00
RECID1:	4.00	8.00	20.00	1.00	2.00	29.00	
COMPLETE:	2.00	1.00	8.00	47.00	1.00	2.00	.00
RECID1:	4.00	7.00	19.00	1.00	2.00	27.00	
COMPLETE:	2.00	1.00	9.00	46.00	1.00	2.00	.00
RECID1:	3.00	6.00	16.00	1.00	2.00	24.00	
COMPLETE:	1.00	2.00	2.00	20.00	2.00	2.00	.00
RECID1:	.00	2.00	3.00	1.00	2.00	4.00	
COMPLETE:	1.00	1.00	.00	16.00	2.00	2.00	.00
RECID1:	1.00	2.00	4.00	2.00	2.00	.00	
COMPLETE:	1.00	2.00	1.00	8.00	2.00	2.00	.00
RECID1:	.00	1.00	2.00	2.00	2.00	5.00	
COMPLETE:	1.00	2.00	.00	5.00	2.00	2.00	.00
RECID1:	1.00	1.00	2.00	2.00	2.00	6.00	
COMPLETE:	1.00	2.00	.00	3.00	2.00	2.00	.00
RECID1:	.00	.00	1.00	2.00	2.00	1.00	
COMPLETE:	1.00	2.00	.00	2.00	2.00	1.00	.00
RECID1:	.00	.00	.00	2.00	2.00	.00	
COMPLETE:	1.00	1.00	.00	2.00	2.00	1.00	.00
RECID1:	.00	.00	.00	2.00	2.00	.00	
COMPLETE:	1.00	3.00	.00	2.00	2.00	1.00	.00
RECID1:	.00	.00	.00	2.00	2.00	.00	
COMPLETE:	1.00	3.00	.00	4.00	2.00	1.00	.00
RECID1:	.00	.00	.00	2.00	2.00	.00	
COMPLETE:	2.00	1.00	8.00	46.00	1.00	2.00	.00
RECID1:	4.00	7.00	15.00	1.00	2.00	26.00	
COMPLETE:	2.00	2.00	9.00	42.00	1.00	2.00	.00
RECID1:	3.00	6.00	17.00	1.00	2.00	23.00	
COMPLETE:	2.00	2.00	.00	3.00	2.00	2.00	.00
RECID1:	.00	.00	.00	2.00	2.00	.00	

COMPLETE:	2.00	1.00	.00	3.00	2.00	2.00	.00
RECID1:	.00	.00	.00	2.00	2.00	.00	
COMPLETE:	2.00	3.00	.00	.00	2.00	2.00	.00
RECID1:	.00	.00	.00	2.00	2.00	.00	
COMPLETE:	1.00	1.00	.00	1.00	1.00	1.00	.00
RECID1:	.00	..	.00	1.00	2.00	.00	
COMPLETE:	1.00	1.00	1.00	2.00	1.00	1.00	.00
RECID1:	1.00	1.00	2.00	2.00	2.00	2.00	
COMPLETE:	1.00	2.00	.00	1.00	2.00	1.00	.00
RECID1:	.00	1.00	1.00	2.00	2.00	1.00	
COMPLETE:	1.00	3.00	.00	.00	2.00	1.00	.00
RECID1:	1.00	1.00	1.00	1.00	2.00	.00	
COMPLETE:	1.00	2.00	.00	.00	2.00	1.00	.00
RECID1:	1.00	1.00	1.00	1.00	2.00	.00	
COMPLETE:	1.00	3.00	.00	2.00	2.00	1.00	.00
RECID1:	1.00	1.00	1.00	1.00	2.00	.00	
COMPLETE:	2.00	2.00	.00	1.00	2.00	1.00	.00
RECID1:	.00	1.00	2.00	2.00	2.00	1.00	
COMPLETE:	2.00	1.00	1.00	3.00	1.00	1.00	.00
RECID1:	1.00	1.00	1.00	2.00	2.00	2.00	
COMPLETE:	1.00	2.00	2.00	1.00	2.00	2.00	.00
RECID1:	.00	.00	1.00	1.00	1.00	.00	
COMPLETE:	2.00	2.00	1.00	3.00	2.00	2.00	.00
RECID1:	1.00	1.00	1.00	2.00	1.00	2.00	
COMPLETE:	2.00	2.00	2.00	4.00	2.00	2.00	.00
RECID1:	1.00	2.00	3.00	2.00	1.00	1.00	
COMPLETE:	1.00	1.00	1.00	3.00	2.00	1.00	.00
RECID1:	.00	1.00	1.00	2.00	1.00	2.00	
COMPLETE:	1.00	1.00	5.00	22.00	1.00	2.00	.00
RECID1:	2.00	6.00	8.00	1.00	1.00	8.00	
COMPLETE:	1.00	2.00	6.00	24.00	1.00	2.00	1.00
RECID1:	3.00	5.00	10.00	1.00	1.00	9.00	
COMPLETE:	2.00	2.00	6.00	24.00	1.00	2.00	1.00
RECID1:	3.00	5.00	11.00	1.00	1.00	9.00	
COMPLETE:	2.00	1.00	8.00	30.00	1.00	2.00	2.00
RECID1:	4.00	6.00	12.00	1.00	1.00	12.00	

COMPLETE:	1.00	2.00	7.00	44.00	1.00	2.00	1.00
RECID1:	4.00	6.00	13.00	1.00	1.00	10.00	
COMPLETE:	1.00	2.00	6.00	30.00	1.00	2.00	.00
RECID1:	3.00	4.00	8.00	1.00	1.00	4.00	
COMPLETE:	1.00	3.00	1.00	2.00	2.00	1.00	.00
RECID1:	.00	.00	.00	2.00	1.00	1.00	
COMPLETE:	2.00	3.00	.00	1.00	2.00	1.00	.00
RECID1:	.00	.00	.00	2.00	1.00	.00	
COMPLETE:	1.00	1.00	.00	2.00	2.00	1.00	.00
RECID1:	1.00	1.00	1.00	1.00	2.00	.00	
COMPLETE:	1.00	1.00	5.00	18.00	1.00	2.00	.00
RECID1:	1.00	3.00	7.00	1.00	2.00	6.00	
COMPLETE:	1.00	1.00	8.00	42.00	1.00	2.00	.00
RECID1:	2.00	6.00	13.00	1.00	2.00	25.00	
COMPLETE:	1.00	1.00	10.00	53.00	1.00	2.00	1.00
RECID1:	4.00	8.00	20.00	1.00	2.00	29.00	
COMPLETE:	2.00	1.00	9.00	46.00	1.00	2.00	.00
RECID1:	3.00	6.00	16.00	1.00	2.00	24.00	
COMPLETE:	1.00	2.00	.00	3.00	2.00	2.00	.00
RECID1:	.00	.00	1.00	2.00	2.00	1.00	
COMPLETE:	1.00	1.00	.00	2.00	2.00	1.00	.00
RECID1:	.00	.00	.00	2.00	2.00	.00	
COMPLETE:	2.00	3.00	.00	.00	2.00	2.00	.00
RECID1:	.00	.00	.00	2.00	2.00	.00	
COMPLETE:	1.00	2.00	2.00	1.00	2.00	2.00	.00
RECID1:	.00	.00	1.00	1.00	1.00	.00	
COMPLETE:	2.00	3.00	.00	1.00	2.00	1.00	.00
RECID1:	.00	.00	2.00	2.00	1.00	.00	
COMPLETE:	1.00	3.00	1.00	2.00	2.00	1.00	.00
RECID1:	.00	.00	.00	2.00	1.00	1.00	
COMPLETE:	2.00	3.00	.00	1.00	2.00	1.00	.00
RECID1:	.00	.00	.00	2.00	1.00	.00	
COMPLETE:	1.00	2.00	6.00	24.00	1.00	2.00	1.00
RECID1:	3.00	5.00	10.00	1.00	1.00	9.00	
COMPLETE:	2.00	2.00	6.00	24.00	1.00	2.00	1.00
RECID1:	3.00	5.00	11.00	1.00	1.00	9.00	

| COMPLETE: | 1.00 | 2.00 | .00 | .00 | 1.00 | 2.00 | .00 |
| RECID1: | .00 | 4.00 | .00 | 2.00 | 1.00 | .00 | |

| COMPLETE: | 1.00 | 2.00 | .00 | 33.00 | 2.00 | 2.00 | .00 |
| RECID1: | .00 | .00 | .00 | 2.00 | 2.00 | .00 | |

| COMPLETE: | 2.00 | 3.00 | .00 | 3.00 | 2.00 | 1.00 | 4.00 |
| RECID1: | .00 | .00 | .00 | 2.00 | 2.00 | 1.00 | |

| COMPLETE: | 2.00 | 2.00 | .00 | .00 | 1.00 | 2.00 | .00 |
| RECID1: | .00 | .00 | 1.00 | 2.00 | 2.00 | .00 | |

| COMPLETE: | 2.00 | 3.00 | .00 | 4.00 | 2.00 | 2.00 | .00 |
| RECID1: | .00 | .00 | 2.00 | 1.00 | 2.00 | .00 | |

| COMPLETE: | 2.00 | 4.00 | .00 | 2.00 | 2.00 | 2.00 | .00 |
| RECID1: | 1.00 | 1.00 | 2.00 | 2.00 | 2.00 | .00 | |

Number of cases read: 60   Number of cases listed: 60

CAPITAL PUNISHMENT SURVEY
Codebook: DEATHPEN.SAV

```
        A              C       E       J               R
        R        C     O     D C F     U       P       E
        G A   B C H      M D R O A     V M P O         L         R S S           S
        U T   E A A C C   M O U N M    E E O L         I         E C E           O             V
        M T   L M R H L I N A O C G H N N L I P R R G   PHR       I       U I
    A E E     I P I O A T A L M R A I I T I T R A A I   E O I S A         S C
    G N N     E U T I S T T C I I N R L A C I A C P O   A O A E L         H T
    E T D     F S Y R S E E O C M G E E L E C Y E E N  RELSCORE T L L X S SUNSCHOO R M

    22 1 2   6 1 2 1 1 1 2 1 2 2 1 2 2 2 1 2 3 1 2 5      7     2 1 1 1 2    2     1 1
    20 2 4   7 2 3 5 2 4 2 2 2 1 1 1 2 2 1 2 4 2 2 3     20     1 1 1 2 2    2     2 1
    18 1 2  10 1 1 1 1 1 1 1 1 2 1 1 1 1 1 2 2 2 2 1      3     2 1 1 2 2    1     1 1
    21 2 4   4 1 4 1 1 3 4 2 2 2 1 1 2 2 1 3 3 2 2 3     18     2 1 1 2 2    4     2 2
    21 2 3   0 1 2 1 1 1 1 2 3 2 2 2 2 2 3 2 2 2 1       4     2 1 2 2 1    1     1 2
    20 1 2   8 1 5 1 1 1 1 3 2 1 2 1 2 1 2 1 2 1 3       8     2 1 1 1 1    2     1 1
    19 2 3   2 1 3 1 2 1 3 2 3 2 2 2 2 2 2 3 2 2 1       8     1 2 1 2 1    1     1 2
    24 2 2   0 1 1 1 2 1 1 2 3 2 2 2 2 2 2 3 1 2 2 4     1     2 1 2 2 1    1     1 2
    21 2 3   8 1 2 1 2 1 3 1 2 2 1 1 . 2 1 3 4 2 1 1    10     1 1 1 2 2    2     1 1
    20 2 4   1 3 1 4 1 3 4 2 2 2 2 2 2 2 2 3 4 2 2 3    22     2 1 1 2 3    2     4 2
    20 2 3   3 1 2 1 2 1 3 2 2 2 2 2 2 1 2 4 2 2 3      11     2 1 1 2 2    1     3 1
    22 1 3  10 1 1 2 2 1 3 1 . 1 1 1 1 1 1 . 2 2 2 3     8     2 1 1 2 2    2     1 1
    21 1 2  11 1 1 2 1 1 1 1 1 1 1 2 1 3 3 2 1 5        4     1 1 1 2 1    1     1 1
    22 2 4  10 2 3 1 1 1 2 1 1 1 1 1 1 1 2 1 1 3 2 1 5  12     1 1 1 1 3    1     2 1
    20 2 2   2 1 1 1 2 1 1 2 1 2 2 . 2 2 1 3 4 2 2 1     4     2 1 1 1 1    1     1 .
    19 2 3   6 1 1 1 1 2 2 2 1 2 1 1 2 1 2 2 2 2 3       7     2 1 1 2 2    2     2 1
    20 1 4   5 1 4 1 1 3 5 2 1 2 2 1 2 1 2 2 4 2 2 1    16     2 1 1 2 2    1     1 1
    32 1 4   9 1 3 1 2 2 3 1 2 1 2 2 2 1 1 2 3 2 1 1    14     1 2 1 1 3    2     2 1
    41 2 3   4 2 3 2 2 2 3 2 2 . 2 1 2 2 . 2 4 2 2 1    15     1 2 1 2 3    1     2 1
    43 2 5   9 3 4 5 1 4 5 1 2 1 2 1 1 2 1 3 5 1 1 1    31     1 2 1 1 4    3     3 1
     . 2 2   5 1 3 1 2 1 2 2 2 1 1 2 2 2 1 3 4 2 2 1     7     2 2 1 2 1    1     1 1
    30 1 3  11 1 1 1 2 1 3 1 2 1 2 1 1 1 1 1 2 3 2 1 3   7     . 2 1 1 2    1     1 1
    24 2 2   0 1 1 1 2 1 1 3 2 2 2 2 2 2 3 3 2 2 1       3     2 2 2 2 1    1     1 2
    25 2 2   6 1 3 2 1 1 3 2 2 1 1 2 1 2 1 3 4 2 2 1    11     2 2 1 2 3    1     1 1
    26 . 4   6 3 2 1 2 1 3 . 2 1 . . 1 . 1 . 1 2 5 2 . 3 17     1 2 1 2 4    3     3 1
    24 . 2   4 2 2 2 2 2 1 2 2 2 . 1 2 2 . 1 2 2 1 3     8     2 2 1 2 2    1     2 1
    22 2 5   5 1 1 1 2 1 2 2 2 2 1 1 1 2 2 2 5 2 2 3    10     2 2 1 2 2    1     1 1
    21 2 5   7 1 1 1 2 1 4 1 2 2 1 . 2 2 1 2 4 2 1 3    14     1 2 1 2 3    1     3 1
    22 2 3   0 1 2 1 2 1 4 2 3 2 2 2 2 2 2 2 5 2 2 3    11     2 2 2 2 1    1     2 2
    25 2 4   3 1 2 5 2 1 2 . 2 1 . . . . . 1 3 5 2 2 3  20     2 2 1 2 3    4     3 1
    43 2 5   7 1 2 1 2 3 5 2 2 1 1 2 2 1 1 1 5 2 2 3    24     1 2 1 2 3    4     5 1
    26 1 3  12 1 1 1 2 1 3 1 1 1 1 1 1 1 1 1 3 4 2 1 3   9     1 2 1 2 1    1     3 1
    24 1 2   7 1 1 1 2 1 1 2 2 2 2 1 2 2 1 3 4 2 1 1     4     1 2 1 2 1    1     1 1
    39 2 3   0 1 2 1 2 2 3 2 2 2 2 2 2 2 2 2 3 2 2 3    10     2 2 2 2 2    1     2 2
    35 2 5   0 1 5 2 2 4 5 2 3 2 2 2 2 2 2 3 4 2 2 1    27     2 2 2 2 4    3     4 2
    23 2 2   7 1 1 1 2 1 1 1 2 1 1 1 1 2 2 1 3 2 2 1     2     2 1 2 1 1    1     1 1
    21 2 4   0 1 4 1 1 1 4 2 3 2 2 2 2 2 2 3 5 2 2 1    14     2 2 2 2 2    1     1 2
    22 2 5   2 3 3 5 2 5 4 2 2 2 1 2 2 2 2 2 2 2 2 1    28     2 2 1 2 4    1     5 2
    30 2 1   3 1 4 . 1 1 1 1 1 . 2 1 2 2 2 . . . 1 2 2 4 3     2 2 2 2 1    1     1 2
    27 2 5   9 1 4 1 1 2 5 2 1 1 1 1 1 2 1 1 3 2 1 1    19     1 2 1 1 4    2     2 1
    22 2 3   3 1 5 1 2 2 2 2 3 2 2 2 2 2 1 3 3 2 2 3    11     1 2 1 2 2    1     1 2
    40 2 3   8 1 2 2 2 3 2 1 2 . 1 1 1 2 1 2 5 2 1 3    16     2 2 1 1 2    3     3 1
    27 2 2   0 1 3 1 1 1 1 2 3 . 2 2 2 2 2 3 3 2 2 1     5     2 2 2 2 1    1     1 .
```

```
      A                 C     E        J              R
      R        C        O  DCF         U        P     E
      G A  B C H     M D R O A      V M P O      L              R S S      S O                V
      U T  E A A C C H O U N M      E E O L      L I            E C E      O C          U I
      M T  L M R H L I N A O C G H N N L I P R R G              P H R      I            S C
      A E E I P I O A T A L M R A I I T I T R A A I             E O I S A               H T
      G N N E U T I S T T C I I N R L A C I A C P O             A O A E L               E I
      E T D F S Y R S E E O C M G E E L E C Y E E N  RELSCORE   T L L X S  SUNSCHOO     R M

52 2 5  6 1 2 3 2 1 4 1 1 1 2 1 2 2 2 1 2 4 2 2 1     13        2 2 1 2 1     1          1 1
46 2 3  3 1 3 1 2 4 4 2 1 2 2 2 2 1 1 1 4 2 2 3       22        2 2 1 2 3     5          4 2
20 1 5 12 5 2 1 2 1 5 1 2 1 1 1 1 1 2 3 2 1 1         15        1 1 1 1 1     1          1 1
20 2 1  7 1 2 1 2 2 3 2 1 1 1 1 1 2 1 3 3 2 2 3        9        2 1 1 2 2     1          3 1
20 2 2  6 1 1 1 1 1 1 1 2 1 2 1 1 2 2 2 2 2 1          3        2 1 1 2 2     1          1 1
22 2 4  8 4 2 5 2 2 4 1 1 1 1 1 1 1 2 1 2 4 2 2 1     19        2 1 1 2 2     1          1 1
20 2 2  1 2 2 1 2 1 2 2 2 2 2 2 2 2 3 2 2 2 1          7        2 1 1 2 2     2          1 2
21 1 4 10 1 1 1 2 1 2 1 2 1 1 1 1 1 1 3 3 2 2 1        6        2 1 1 2 1     1          1 1
19 2 5  7 3 1 4 2 2 2 1 1 2 1 2 2 1 1 1 3 2 1 1       14        2 1 1 2 1     1          2 1
21 2 4  0 5 5 1 2 3 1 2 3 2 2 2 2 2 2 3 4 2 2 5       18        2 1 2 1 3     1          1 2
22 1 2 12 1 1 1 1 1 1 1 1 2 1 1 1 1 2 1 2 1 3          1        1 1 1 1 1     1          1 1
20 2 3  1 1 1 1 2 1 3 2 2 2 2 2 2 2 2 2 2 2 3          7        2 1 1 2 2     1          2 2
21 1 5  8 1 4 1 2 2 4 1 2 1 1 1 2 2 1 2 5 2 2 5       21        2 1 1 2 3     4          2 1
19 2 3  7 1 3 2 2 2 2 2 2 1 1 1 2 2 1 3 3 2 1 3       13        2 1 1 2 2     3          2 1
20 2 2  3 1 3 1 1 1 2 2 3 2 1 2 2 2 1 3 2 2 2 3        7        2 1 1 2 1     2          2 2
19 . 2  8 1 2 1 2 2 1 1 2 . 1 1 2 2 1 2 1 2 1 4        3        1 1 1 2 1     1          1 1
20 2 3  6 1 1 3 1 1 2 2 1 1 2 1 1 2 2 1 2 3 2 2 3     12        1 1 1 2 2     3          3 1
22 2 2  6 1 2 1 1 1 2 2 2 1 1 1 2 2 2 2 2 2 1          5        2 1 1 1 2     1          1 1
24 1 2  9 1 1 1 2 1 1 1 2 1 1 1 1 2 1 3 2 2 1          3        2 1 1 2 1     1          1 1
21 1 2  9 1 3 1 1 1 1 1 2 1 1 2 1 1 1 1 2 4 2 1 3     8        2 1 1 1 1     2          2 1
21 2 2  3 1 2 1 1 1 1 2 2 2 2 1 2 2 3 3 2 2 3         4        2 1 1 2 1     1          1 1
21 1 1  9 1 3 1 1 1 1 1 2 1 1 1 2 1 1 1 2 2 2 2       2        1 1 1 1 1     1          1 1
23 2 2  8 1 4 1 1 1 1 2 3 1 1 1 1 2 1 3 2 2 2 1       5        1 1 1 2 1     1          1 1
32 2 4  6 1 1 1 2 1 3 1 1 1 1 2 2 2 1 1 4 2 2 3      11        2 1 1 1 2     2          2 1
22 1 2  6 1 3 1 1 1 2 3 2 1 2 2 1 1 1 2 2 2 2 3       5        2 1 1 1 1     1          1 2
21 2 2  6 1 5 1 1 1 2 2 2 1 2 1 2 2 1 3 4 2 1 3      10        2 1 1 2 1     2          1 1
21 2 3  7 1 1 1 2 1 3 1 1 2 1 1 2 1 1 2 3 2 2 1       7        2 1 1 1 2     1          1 1
20 1 2  9 1 1 1 3 2 1 2 1 1 1 1 1 2 2 1 2 1 1 1 2    4        1 1 1 1 1     1          1 1
18 2 4  0 2 3 2 1 2 4 2 2 2 2 2 2 2 2 2 3 2 2 3      16        2 1 2 2 2     2          2 2
21 2 2  4 1 2 1 2 1 1 2 2 2 1 1 2 2 1 2 5 2 2 5       7        2 1 1 2 2     1          1 2
21 2 2  5 1 1 1 2 1 1 2 2 2 2 1 2 2 2 2 2 2 5        3        1 1 1 2 2     1          1 1
20 1 3  9 3 4 1 2 2 2 1 1 2 1 1 1 2 1 1 1 2 1 3     11        2 1 1 2 1     1          2 1
22 2 1  4 1 4 1 1 1 1 1 2 2 1 . 2 2 1 3 1 2 2 4      4        2 1 1 1 1     1          1 2
23 2 3  6 1 1 1 1 2 2 2 1 1 2 2 1 3 1 2 2 2 . 2      2        1 1 1 2 1     1          1 1
23 2 5  0 2 3 2 2 3 5 2 1 2 2 2 2 2 2 1 5 2 2 3     30        2 1 2 1 5     5          5 2
22 1 1 12 1 2 1 2 1 1 1 2 1 1 1 1 1 1 1 1 2 1 3      1        1 1 1 1 1     1          1 1
22 2 2  3 1 2 1 2 1 2 2 2 2 2 2 2 2 1 3 2 2 3        4        2 1 1 2 1     1          1 1
20 1 1  8 1 3 1 1 1 2 2 1 2 1 2 1 2 1 2 1 4         2        1 1 1 1 1     1          1 1
20 2 3  8 3 2 5 2 3 2 1 1 1 1 1 1 2 2 1 3 2 2 1 3  15        1 1 1 1 3     1          1 1
21 1 2  7 1 2 1 1 1 1 1 2 1 1 . 2 2 1 2 1 2 2 4     2        2 1 1 1 1     1          1 1
19 2 5  9 3 4 1 2 2 4 1 1 1 1 1 2 2 1 2 5 2 1 3    20        1 1 1 2 3     1          2 1
18 2 2  7 3 4 2 2 3 2 1 2 1 1 1 2 2 . 3 3 2 2      19        1 1 1 2 2     5          3 1
29 2 1  2 1 1 1 2 1 2 2 2 2 2 2 2 2 1 2 1 2 2 4     0        2 1 1 1 1     1          1 2
20 1 2 12 1 3 1 2 1 1 1 1 1 1 1 1 1 1 1 1 2 2 1 1  4        1 1 1 2 1     1          1 1
```

```
 A
 R                 C       E
 G  A  B C H       O    D C F      J              R
 U  T  E A A C M   M    O U N M    U    V M P O   E
 M  T  L M R H L I N    O C G H N  P    E E O L   L        R S S        S
 A  E E I P I O A T A L C M G E E L A   N N L I P R R G    E C E   C    O              V
 G  N N E U T I S T T C M G E E L E C   R R A C I A C P O  P H R   I    O          U I
 E  T D F S Y R S E E O F M G E E L E C Y E E N RELSCORE   A O A E L  SUNSCHOO       S C
                                                          T L L X S               H T
                                                                                  E I
                                                                                  R M

23 2 4   7 2 5 4 1 4 5 2 3 1 1 1 2 2 1 3 3 2 2 3    27    1 1 1 1 3    2    5 1
20 2 2   5 1 1 1 1 2 2 2 2 2 2 1 1 2 1 2 2 2 2 3     6    1 1 1 1 2    1    2 2
26 2 2   4 1 2 1 1 1 2 2 2 2 1 2 2 1 1 3 2 2 2 1     5    2 1 1 1 2    1    1 2
21 2 2   2 1 1 1 2 1 2 2 1 2 2 2 2 2 2 2 2 2 2 3     4    2 1 1 2 2    1    1 1
26 2 4   3 1 2 1 1 1 4 2 1 2 2 2 2 2 1 2 5 2 2 1    12    1 1 1 1 2    1    1 2
18 1 5   9 1 2 1 2 1 4 1 2 1 1 1 1 2 1 2 5 2 2 1    12    2 1 1 2 1    1    1 1
19 2 1   0 1 1 1 1 1 2 2 2 2 2 2 2 2 2 1 2 2 3       0    2 1 2 1 1    1    1 2
22 1 3  12 2 1 2 1 1 2 1 2 1 1 1 1 1 1 4 2 1 3       8    1 1 1 2 1    1    1 1
22 2 3   5 1 1 1 1 1 2 2 . 1 1 2 2 1 1 4 2 2 3       6    2 2 1 2 2    1    1 1
23 2 2   3 1 1 1 1 2 2 2 2 1 2 2 2 2 2 1 2 2 1       2    2 2 1 2 1    1    1 1
23 1 2   7 1 1 1 2 1 1 1 2 1 1 2 2 1 1 2 2 2 3       2    2 2 1 1 1    1    1 1
23 2 3   2 1 3 1 1 1 2 2 2 2 2 2 2 2 2 4 2 2 1       9    2 2 1 2 2    1    1 1
22 2 2   5 2 2 2 1 2 2 2 2 2 1 1 2 2 2 3 2 2 1       9    1 2 1 2 2    1    1 1
23 1 3   7 2 4 1 2 2 3 1 3 1 1 2 2 2 1 3 3 2 1 3    13    2 2 1 2 2    1    2 1
22 2 3   5 1 2 2 2 1 1 2 2 2 2 1 1 2 2 2 4 2 2 1    10    1 2 1 1 3    1    2 1
21 2 2   3 1 1 1 2 1 2 2 2 2 1 2 2 2 1 2 2 2 1       4    2 2 1 1 2    1    1 2
21 1 2   7 1 1 1 1 1 1 2 1 1 2 1 2 2 2 1 1 5 2 2 1   5    1 2 1 1 1    1    1 1
22 2 4   7 1 2 1 1 2 3 1 2 2 1 2 1 2 1 2 4 2 1 1    11    2 2 1 2 2    1    1 1
22 2 5   4 3 2 2 2 1 4 2 2 2 1 2 2 2 1 2 4 2 2 1    16    2 2 1 2 2    1    2 1
24 2 3   0 1 3 1 1 3 2 1 2 2 2 2 2 3 3 2 2 3        10    2 2 2 2 2    2    1 2
22 2 3   5 1 1 1 1 1 1 2 2 1 1 1 1 1 2 1 2 2 3       3    2 2 1 1 1    1    1 1
21 1 2  11 1 2 1 1 1 1 2 2 1 1 1 1 1 1 2 2 1 1       3    1 2 1 1 1    1    1 1
21 1 2  12 1 1 1 1 1 1 1 1 1 1 1 1 1 1 2 2 1 3       2    1 2 1 1 1    1    1 1
29 2 1   6 1 3 1 1 1 1 2 2 1 2 1 2 2 2 2 5 4 1 5     6    1 2 1 2 1    1    1 1
21 2 5   6 2 5 2 1 2 2 2 2 1 1 1 1 2 2 3 4 2 2 1    18    2 2 1 2 2    2    2 1
22 2 2   7 1 1 1 1 1 1 1 2 1 1 1 2 2 1 2 1 2 2 .     1    2 2 1 1 1    1    1 1
22 2 3   2 1 1 1 1 3 2 2 2 2 2 2 2 2 3 2 2 3         8    2 2 1 2 3    1    1 2
25 2 5   4 1 2 4 2 2 5 2 2 2 2 1 2 2 1 1 5 2 2 1    18    2 2 1 2 2    1    1 1
19 2 5   5 2 2 1 2 3 1 1 1 2 2 2 2 2 1 4 2 1 1      18    1 2 1 1 2    5    3 2
18 2 5   7 1 2 1 2 2 3 2 2 2 1 1 1 2 1 2 3 2 1 1    12    2 2 1 2 2    1    2 1
20 2 2   7 1 2 1 1 1 1 1 1 1 1 2 1 1 2 2 5 2 3       4    2 2 1 1 1    1    2 1
19 2 3   7 1 2 1 2 1 3 2 2 2 1 1 2 2 1 2 2 2 1 3     7    1 2 1 2 2    1    1 1
19 2 4   2 3 2 3 2 2 3 2 2 2 2 2 2 2 2 3 2 1 1      16    2 2 1 2 3    1    2 2
19 2 4   4 3 2 3 2 3 3 2 1 2 2 1 1 2 1 1 4 2 2 3    21    2 2 1 1 3    3    3 2
19 2 5   1 5 3 1 1 2 5 2 2 2 2 2 2 2 2 1 5 2 2 5    29    2 2 1 2 5    4    4 2
19 1 2  10 1 1 1 1 2 1 1 1 1 1 1 2 1 2 1 2 2 1       2    1 2 1 1 1    1    1 1
19 2 3   0 1 1 1 2 1 2 2 2 2 2 2 2 2 2 3 2 2 3       5    2 2 2 2 1    1    1 2
19 2 4   1 1 1 1 2 1 3 2 1 2 2 2 2 2 2 2 4 2 2 1    10    2 2 2 1 2    1    2 1
18 1 4  10 1 2 2 2 2 4 1 2 1 1 1 1 1 1 1 4 2 2 3    13    2 2 1 1 2    1    1 1
21 1 2   8 1 1 1 2 1 1 1 1 2 1 1 1 1 2 1 1 1 1 2 2 3 3    2 2 1 1 2    1    1 1
19 1 1   8 1 1 1 2 1 1 2 1 1 1 1 1 1 1 2 2 1 3       1    2 2 1 1 1    1    1 1
22 2 3   7 1 2 1 1 2 4 2 3 1 1 1 1 2 2 1 2 4 4 2 1  12    1 2 1 1 2    2    1 1
19 1 2   8 1 1 1 2 1 3 1 2 1 1 1 1 1 2 1 2 2 1       4    2 2 1 1 2    1    1 1
18 1 2   7 1 1 1 2 1 1 1 2 1 1 1 2 2 1 2 3 2 2 3     3    2 2 1 2 1    1    1 1
```

```
    A               C       E       J               R
    R           C   O   D C F   U       P           E
    G A   B C H     M D R O A   V M P O         L                       S
    U T   E A A C C M O U N M   E E O L         I       R S S           O                   V
    M T   L M R H L I N A O C G H N N L I P R R G       E C E   C                           U I
A E E     I P I O A T A L M R A I I T I T R A A I       P H R   I                           S C
G N N     E U T I S T T C I I N R L A C I A C P O       E O I S A                           H T
E T D     F S Y R S E E O C M G E E L E C Y E E N RELSCORE T L L X S SUNSCHOO               R M

21 1 2   9 1 1 1 2 1 2 2 1 1 2 1 1 2 1 2 3 2 1 3     6   1 2 1 1 2     1     2 1
19 2 2   8 1 1 1 1 1 1 1 2 1 1 1 1 2 1 3 2 2 1 3     2   2 2 1 2 1     1     1 1
20 2 2   4 1 1 1 2 1 1 2 2 2 2 2 1 2 1 3 2 2 2 3     2   2 2 1 1 1     1     1 1
19 1 4  10 1 2 1 1 4 4 1 1 1 1 2 1 1 1 2 4 2 1 3    17   2 2 1 1 3     1     3 1
19 1 2  10 1 2 1 2 1 1 1 1 2 1 1 1 1 2 2 2 2 3      4   2 2 1 2 2      1     1 1
19 2 5   9 1 2 1 1 3 4 1 1 1 1 1 1 1 2 3 2 1 1     19   2 2 1 1 5      1     4 1
18 2 4   5 1 1 1 1 1 2 2 2 1 1 2 2 1 2 2 2 2 1      4   2 2 1 2 1      1     1 1
19 2 3   4 1 1 1 1 1 2 2 1 2 2 2 2 1 2 2 2 2 1 3     4   1 2 1 1 1     1     1 2
22 2 2   8 1 1 1 2 1 1 1 2 1 2 1 1 1 1 2 1 2 2 4     1   2 2 1 1 1     1     1 1
28 1 5  10 1 3 1 2 1 4 1 1 1 1 1 1 1 1 5 2 2 5    17   2 2 1 1 3       1     3 1
24 2 5   3 4 3 2 2 3 3 2 2 2 2 1 2 2 1 2 4 2 2 1    22   2 2 1 1 4      1     3 2
18 1 5  10 1 1 4 2 1 3 1 2 1 1 1 1 . 1 2 3 2 1 5    21   2 2 1 1 3      5     5 1
```

Number of cases read: 143   Number of cases listed: 143

ALCOHOL STUDY
Codebook: ALCO.SAV

AGE	AUNT	CLASS	DESTROY	DRINK	DRUGS	DUI	FIGHT	GPA	OBSCENE	OFTEN	RACE	RESIDENC	SEX	SHOPLIFT	STOLENPP	STOLENSS	TYPE
23	5	4	2	1	2	1	1	3	2	5	1	2	1	2	1	2	1
22	5	4	2	1	1	1	2	3	1	4	1	2	2	1	2	1	1
22	3	4	2	2	2	2	2	2	2	3	1	1	1	2	2	2	1
21	4	4	2	2	2	2	2	2	1	4	1	2	2	1	2	2	1
22	2	4	2	1	2	2	1	3	2	3	1	2	2	2	2	2	1
.	.	4	2	2	2	2	2	1	2	.	1	2	2	2	2	2	.
21	3	4	2	1	1	2	1	2	2	3	1	2	2	1	2	2	1
21	2	4	2	1	2	2	2	2	2	1	1	3	2	2	2	2	2
22	.	4	2	2	2	2	2	2	2	.	1	2	2	2	2	2	.
40	1	4	2	1	2	2	2	1	2	2	1	2	2	2	2	2	1
21	4	4	2	1	2	1	2	2	2	2	1	1	2	2	2	2	1
21	3	4	2	1	2	1	1	2	2	2	1	2	2	2	2	2	1
21	5	4	1	1	1	1	2	4	1	4	1	2	2	2	2	2	1
22	3	4	2	1	1	1	2	2	2	3	1	2	2	2	2	2	1
22	2	4	2	1	2	1	2	2	2	4	1	2	2	2	2	2	1
21	2	4	2	1	2	2	2	3	2	1	1	1	2	2	2	2	3
22	1	4	2	1	2	1	2	3	2	3	1	3	2	2	2	2	3
22	2	4	2	1	2	1	2	1	2	3	1	2	2	2	2	2	3
21	2	3	2	1	2	1	2	3	2	2	1	1	2	2	2	2	2
23	4	4	2	1	2	1	2	4	2	4	1	1	2	2	2	2	1
19	1	1	2	1	2	1	2	3	1	3	1	1	1	1	1	2	1
19	2	1	2	1	2	1	2	3	2	3	1	1	2	2	2	2	3
18	3	1	2	1	2	2	2	1	2	3	1	1	2	1	2	2	1
19	3	1	2	1	1	1	2	3	2	3	1	1	2	2	2	1	1
20	2	2	2	1	2	2	2	5	2	3	2	1	1	2	2	2	1
19	3	1	2	1	2	2	2	4	2	4	1	1	2	2	2	2	1
19	.	2	2	2	2	2	2	4	2	.	2	1	1	2	2	2	.
19	4	1	1	1	1	1	2	2	2	4	1	1	2	2	2	2	1
19	3	1	2	1	2	2	2	4	1	4	1	1	2	2	2	2	1
18	3	1	1	1	1	1	1	2	1	4	1	1	2	1	1	2	1
20	4	2	1	1	1	1	1	4	2	4	1	2	1	2	2	2	1
20	1	2	2	1	2	2	2	3	2	1	1	1	2	2	2	2	1
19	4	2	2	1	2	1	2	3	2	4	1	2	2	2	2	2	1
20	4	2	2	1	1	2	1	5	2	5	1	2	2	1	1	1	1
21	2	4	1	1	1	1	2	4	2	2	1	1	1	2	2	1	1
33	.	4	2	2	2	2	2	3	2	.	1	3	2	2	2	2	.
21	2	3	2	1	2	2	2	3	2	1	4	1	2	1	2	2	2
21	5	4	2	1	1	1	2	3	2	4	1	2	2	1	1	2	1
.	2	4	2	1	2	2	2	1	2	2	1	2	2	2	2	2	1
22	4	4	2	1	1	1	2	3	2	4	1	2	2	2	2	1	1
32	.	4	2	2	2	2	2	3	2	.	1	2	2	2	2	2	.
21	4	4	2	1	1	1	2	3	2	5	1	2	2	2	2	2	1
21	.	4	2	2	2	2	2	3	2	.	1	3	2	2	2	2	.
22	2	4	2	1	2	2	1	2	2	3	1	3	2	2	2	1	1
22	2	4	1	1	2	2	2	2	1	2	1	2	2	2	2	1	3

AGE	AMOUNT	CLASS	DESTROY	DRINK	DRUGS	DUI	FIGHT	GPA	OBSCENE	OFTEN	RACE	RESIDENC	SEX	SHOPLIFT	STOLENPP	STOLENSS	TYPE
31	.	4	2	2	2	2	2	2	2	.	1	4	2	2	2	2	.
21	2	4	2	1	2	2	2	2	2	1	1	2	2	2	2	2	2
.	2	4	2	1	1	2	2	3	2	2	1	2	2	2	2	2	3
21	3	4	1	1	2	1	2	2	1	2	1	2	2	2	1	1	1
21	3	4	2	1	1	1	2	3	1	4	1	2	2	2	2	1	1
20	4	3	1	1	1	2	2	2	2	4	1	2	1	2	2	1	1
19	4	2	2	1	1	1	1	2	1	4	1	2	2	2	2	2	1
38	2	4	1	1	1	1	1	1	2	3	1	4	2	2	2	2	1
20	5	2	2	1	2	1	1	3	2	4	1	1	1	2	1	2	1
20	2	3	2	1	2	2	2	1	2	3	1	2	2	2	2	2	1
20	.	3	2	1	2	2	2	1	2	3	1	2	2	2	2	2	1
21	2	4	2	1	2	1	2	2	2	1	1	2	2	2	2	2	3
18	.	1	1	2	2	2	2	3	2	.	1	1	1	2	1	2	.
19	2	1	2	1	2	2	2	3	2	1	1	1	2	2	2	2	2
19	.	1	2	2	2	2	2	1	2	.	1	1	2	2	2	2	.
19	.	1	2	2	2	2	2	2	2	.	1	1	2	2	2	2	.
18	.	1	2	2	2	2	2	2	2	.	1	1	2	2	2	2	.
27	2	1	2	1	1	1	2	1	2	2	1	4	2	2	2	2	2
18	.	1	2	2	2	2	2	1	2	.	1	1	2	2	2	2	.
18	2	1	2	1	2	2	2	2	2	1	1	1	2	2	2	2	1
18	.	1	2	1	1	1	2	3	2	4	1	1	2	1	1	2	1
18	2	1	2	1	2	2	2	3	2	2	1	1	2	2	2	2	1
18	2	1	2	1	2	2	2	2	2	2	1	1	2	2	2	2	1
18	.	1	2	2	2	2	2	1	2	.	1	3	2	2	2	2	.
19	3	1	2	1	2	2	2	3	2	4	1	1	2	2	2	2	3
18	2	1	2	1	2	1	2	2	2	2	1	1	2	2	2	2	1
19	3	1	2	1	1	2	2	3	2	2	1	3	1	2	2	2	1
19	.	1	2	2	2	2	2	3	2	.	1	1	2	2	2	2	.
19	3	2	2	1	1	2	2	2	1	6	1	1	2	2	2	2	1
21	1	3	2	1	2	2	2	3	2	1	1	2	2	2	2	2	3
22	1	4	2	1	2	2	2	4	2	2	2	1	1	2	2	2	3
18	2	1	2	1	2	1	2	1	2	4	1	1	2	2	1	2	1
19	2	2	2	1	1	2	1	3	2	3	1	1	2	2	1	1	1
21	3	3	2	1	1	2	2	4	2	4	1	1	1	2	2	2	3
20	.	3	2	2	2	2	2	4	2	.	2	1	2	2	2	2	.
21	2	3	2	1	1	1	2	3	2	4	1	2	2	2	2	2	1
19	3	2	2	1	2	1	2	3	1	4	1	1	2	2	1	1	1
21	3	3	1	1	2	1	2	5	2	3	1	2	1	2	1	2	1
19	3	2	2	1	2	1	2	2	2	4	1	2	2	2	2	2	1
28	2	2	2	1	2	2	2	1	2	4	1	2	2	2	2	2	2
30	2	2	2	1	2	2	1	3	2	1	1	3	1	2	2	2	2
21	1	2	2	1	2	2	2	2	2	1	1	2	2	2	2	2	2
21	.	3	2	2	2	2	2	2	2	.	1	1	2	2	2	2	.
20	2	2	2	1	2	2	2	1	2	1	1	2	2	2	2	2	1
28	.	3	2	2	2	2	2	4	2	.	3	3	2	2	2	2	.
19	3	2	2	1	2	1	2	3	2	3	1	1	2	2	2	2	1

AGE	AMOUNT	CLASS	DESTROY	DRINK	DRUGS	FIDUI	FIGHT	GPA	OBSCENE	OFTEN	RACE	RESIDENC	SEX	SHOPLIFT	STOLENPP	STOLENSS	TYPE
21	2	2	2	1	2	2	2	5	2	1	2	1	2	2	2	2	3
19	2	2	2	1	2	2	2	1	2	1	1	1	2	2	2	2	2
.	.	1	2	2	2	2	2	3	2	.	5	4	1	2	2	2	.
19	2	1	2	1	2	2	2	3	1	3	1	1	2	2	2	2	1
19	1	1	2	1	2	2	2	4	2	2	4	1	2	2	2	1	1
18	.	1	1	2	2	2	2	3	2	.	1	1	2	1	1	1	.
18	4	1	2	1	2	2	2	4	2	3	1	1	1	2	2	1	3
20	5	2	1	1	1	1	2	4	2	4	1	1	2	2	2	2	1
18	2	1	2	1	2	1	2	2	2	3	1	1	2	2	2	2	1
19	5	1	2	1	1	1	2	1	1	5	1	1	1	1	2	1	3
19	4	1	1	1	2	1	1	5	1	4	1	1	1	1	2	1	1
19	4	1	2	1	2	1	2	4	2	3	1	1	2	2	2	2	1
19	.	2	2	2	2	2	2	3	2	.	1	3	2	2	1	2	.
18	.	1	2	2	2	2	2	3	2	.	1	1	2	2	1	2	.
21	3	3	2	1	1	1	1	2	2	4	5	1	1	2	2	1	1
21	2	3	2	1	1	1	2	1	2	3	1	2	2	2	2	2	1
18	3	1	2	1	2	2	2	1	2	4	1	1	2	2	2	2	1
19	5	1	1	1	1	1	1	7	2	4	1	1	1	1	2	1	1
21	3	4	2	1	1	1	2	3	2	3	1	2	2	2	2	1	1
18	3	1	2	1	2	2	2	4	2	3	1	1	2	2	2	2	1
22	4	4	1	1	1	1	1	2	1	4	1	2	1	1	1	1	1
21	.	4	2	2	2	2	2	3	2	.	1	1	2	2	2	2	.
32	1	4	2	1	2	2	2	1	2	1	1	4	2	2	2	2	3
20	3	2	2	1	1	1	2	1	2	2	1	1	2	1	2	2	2
22	1	4	2	1	1	2	2	4	2	1	1	4	2	2	2	2	3
.	2	3	2	1	2	2	2	3	2	2	1	1	2	2	2	2	1
40	.	5	2	2	2	2	2	1	2	.	1	2	2	2	2	2	.
20	2	3	2	1	2	1	2	3	2	2	1	1	2	2	2	2	1
22	2	4	2	1	2	2	2	1	2	4	3	3	1	2	2	2	1
31	3	4	2	1	1	1	2	2	2	3	1	4	1	2	2	2	1
.	2	3	2	1	1	2	2	2	2	3	1	2	2	2	2	2	1
21	1	3	2	1	2	2	2	2	2	1	1	1	2	2	2	2	2
21	3	3	2	1	1	1	1	4	1	4	1	1	1	2	2	2	1
.	2	3	2	1	2	2	2	1	2	1	1	4	2	2	2	2	2
20	4	1	2	1	1	2	2	3	2	4	1	1	2	2	2	2	3
19	5	2	2	1	2	2	1	4	2	4	1	1	1	2	2	1	1
19	3	1	2	1	1	2	2	4	2	3	1	1	1	2	2	1	3
19	4	2	2	1	2	1	2	3	2	4	1	1	1	2	2	1	1
20	3	3	2	1	2	1	2	4	2	1	1	1	1	2	2	1	1
18	2	3	2	2	2	2	2	1	2	3	1	1	1	2	2	2	2
19	1	2	2	1	2	2	2	1	2	1	1	2	2	2	2	2	2
20	2	3	2	1	2	2	2	3	2	2	1	2	2	2	2	2	3
18	.	1	1	1	1	1	1	4	1	3	1	1	1	1	1	1	3
18	2	1	2	1	2	1	1	2	2	3	1	1	1	2	1	2	3
25	2	1	2	1	2	2	2	2	2	3	1	3	1	2	2	2	3
18	1	1	2	1	2	2	2	3	2	1	1	3	2	2	2	2	2

AGE	AMOUNT	CLASS	DESTROY	DRINK	DRUGS	DUI	FIGHT	GPA	OBSCENE	OFTEN	RACE	RESIDENC	SEX	SHOPLIFT	STOLENPP	STOLENSS	TYPE
18	1	1	2	1	2	2	2	2	2	1	1	1	2	2	2	2	2
20	.	2	2	2	2	2	2	2	2	.	1	2	1	2	2	2	.
19	.	1	2	2	2	2	2	3	2	.	1	1	2	2	2	2	.
25	.	5	2	2	2	2	2	1	2	.	1	3	1	2	2	2	.
25	3	1	2	1	2	2	2	3	2	2	1	2	1	2	2	2	3
28	.	5	2	2	2	2	2	2	2	.	1	3	1	2	2	2	.
22	2	3	2	1	1	2	2	4	2	3	1	1	2	2	2	2	1
20	.	2	1	2	2	2	1	3	1	.	1	1	1	2	1	2	.
18	.	1	2	2	2	2	2	3	2	.	1	1	2	2	2	2	.
19	1	1	2	1	2	2	2	3	2	1	1	2	2	2	2	2	2
19	.	1	2	2	2	2	2	2	1	.	1	1	1	2	2	2	.
18	2	1	2	1	2	2	2	1	2	1	1	1	1	2	2	2	1
18	3	1	2	1	2	2	2	2	2	1	1	1	1	2	2	2	1
18	3	1	1	1	2	2	1	1	1	2	1	1	1	2	2	1	1
18	.	1	2	2	2	2	2	3	1	.	1	1	1	2	2	2	.
18	.	1	2	2	2	2	2	3	2	.	1	3	2	2	2	2	.
19	2	2	2	1	2	2	2	3	2	2	1	1	2	2	2	2	3
19	2	1	2	1	2	2	2	3	1	1	1	1	2	2	2	2	3
18	.	1	2	2	2	2	2	3	2	.	1	1	1	2	2	2	.
20	3	3	2	1	2	2	2	3	2	3	1	1	1	2	2	2	1
19	.	1	2	2	2	2	2	2	2	.	1	1	2	2	2	2	.
19	.	1	2	2	2	2	2	2	2	.	1	1	2	2	2	2	.
26	1	5	2	1	2	2	2	1	2	1	1	2	2	2	2	2	1
19	2	1	2	1	2	2	2	3	2	2	1	1	2	2	2	2	3
18	.	1	2	2	2	2	2	2	2	.	5	1	2	2	2	2	.

Number of cases read: 162   Number of cases listed: 162

RACISM STUDY
Codebook: RACISM.SAV

The variables are listed in the following order:

LINE   1: ACADABIL AFROAMER AGE AMBITION AMERICAN ASSOCIAT CLASS COURSES DISCRIM
           EDUC EQTREAT FRIENDS HATECRIM HISCHOOL HUMAN INTAMER INTELL JEWISH
           MARRIAGE NEIGHBOR NOEDUC NOINTEL NOMOTIV OPPORTUN ORIENTAL PARVIEW
           POLAFFIL PREJ1 PREJ2 PREJ3 PREJ4 PREJUDIC PSYCHRAC

LINE   2: RACE RACETHNI RELATION RESIDENC SEX SOCCLUB SUPERSTI TRUST YOURVIEW

File: SPSS/PC+

ACADABIL: 2 1 18 2 1 1 1 7 2 2 1 25 1 2 1 1 2 1 1 1 2 2\2 1 1 0 2   4 0   4 0 1 1
    RACE: 1 1 1 3 1 1 2 2 0

ACADABIL: 2 2 18 2 1 1 1 0 1 2 1 60 1 2 2 2 2 2 1 1 2 2 2 1 2 4 1   4 0   4 1 1 2
    RACE: 1 2 1 4 1 1 2 2 0

ACADABIL: 2 2 22 2 1 2 4 1 2 2 1 30 1 2 2 2 2 1 1 1 1 2 2 1 2 2 3   6 0   6 1 2 2
    RACE: 1 2 2 1 1 1 2 2 2

ACADABIL: 2 2 20 1 1 2 2 0 1 2 1 10 1 3 2 2 2 2 1 1 1 2 1 1 2 3 2   7 2   4 1 1 2
    RACE: 2 2 1 1 2 1 1 2 1

ACADABIL: 2 2 20 2 1 2 2 0 1 2 1   1 1 2 2 2 2 2 5 1 2 2 2 1 2 4 1   9 0   4 1 1 2
    RACE: 1 2 1 4 2 1 2 2 1

ACADABIL: 2 2 20 2 1 1 2 0 1 2 1   2 1 2 2 2 2 2 1 1 1 2 2 2 2 3 1   4 0   8 0 2 2
    RACE: 1 2 3 4 2 1 2 2 0

ACADABIL: 2 2 19 2 1 2 1 0 1 2 1   5 1 2 2 2 2 2 1 1 1 2 2 1 2 3 3   5 0   4 0 1 2
    RACE: 1 2 1 4 2 1 2 2 2

ACADABIL: 2 2 19 1 1 2 1 0 2 1 1   5 3 2 2 2 2 2 3 1 1 2 1 4 2 2 1   8 3   9 1 1 2
    RACE: 1 2 1 4 2 2 1 2 1

ACADABIL: 1 2 23 1 1 2 4 0 2 1 1 70 1 2 2 2 2 2 1 3 1 2 2 1 2 2 3   5 4   5 1 1 2
    RACE: 4 2 2 4 2 1 1 2 0

ACADABIL: 1 2 20 1 1 3 2 0 2 1 1   5 2 5 2 2 2 2 3 1 2 2 1 1 2 1 1   8 3   6 3 2 2
    RACE: 1 2 1 3 2 1 2 2 4

ACADABIL: 2 2 19 1 1 2 2 0 1 2 1   5 1 1 2 2 2 2 3 1 1 2 2 1 2 4 3   9 3   7 0 2 2
    RACE: 1 2 3 3 2 3 1 1 3

ACADABIL: 2 2 19 1 1 3 2 0 2 1 1   5 3 1 2 2 2 2 4 1 1 2 2 4 2 5 2   9 2 13 1 3 2
    RACE: 1 2 3 3 2 1 2 2 4

ACADABIL: 2 2 19 1 1 3 2 0 1 1 1   5 1 1 2 2 1 2 3 1 2 2 1 1 2 5 1   8 3   5 2 1 2
    RACE: 1 2 2 3 2 1 2 2 3

ACADABIL: 2 2 18 2 1 3 1 0 1 1 2 20 1 1 2 2 2 2 2 1 1 2 2 2 2 2 1 10 2   7 0 2 2
    RACE: 1 2 2 3 2 3 1 2 1

ACADABIL: 2 2 18 2 1 3 1 0 2 2 1 10 1 2 2 2 2 4 1 2 2 2 1 2 4 3 11 1   6 2 2 2
    RACE: 1 2 2 3 2 3 1 2 1

ACADABIL: 2 2 19 1 1 2 2 0 2 1 1 20 2 2 2 2 2 2 3 2 1 2 1 2 2 4 1   7 3   9 2 2 2
    RACE: 1 2 3 2 2 1 1 2 2

ACADABIL: 2 2 23 2 1 1 4 1 1 1 1   5 1 2 1 2 2 2 2 1 1 2 1 1 2 3 2   5 2   4 1 1 2
    RACE: 5 2 1 2 2 1 1 2 1

ACADABIL: 2 2 19 2 1 2 1 0 1 2 1 20 1 2 2 2 2 2 2 4 2 2 2 1 2 0 2   6 0   4 1 1 2

```
RACE: 1 2 1 2 2 1 2 2 0
ACADABIL: 2 2 18 2 1 1 1 0 2 1 1 50 1 5 2 2 2 2 1 2 1 2 1 2 2 5 2  4 2  9 1 2 2
RACE: 1 2 4 2 2 1 1 2 0
ACADABIL: 2 2 21 2 1 3 2 0 1 1 1  5 1 2 2 2 2 2 1 1 1 2 2 2 2 2 4  6 2  9 0 3 2
RACE: 1 2 3 4 2 1 1 2 0
ACADABIL: 2 2 21 1 1 2 2 1 2 2 1 40 1 2 1 2 2 2 2 1 1 1 2 2 1 2 0 1  5 1  5 1 1 2
RACE: 2 2 2 1 1 1 2 2 0
ACADABIL: 2 2 20 2 1 3 3 0 1 2 1  5 1 2 2 2 2 2 1 1 1 2 2 2 2 3 4  6 1  8 0 2 2
RACE: 1 2 3 2 1 1 1 2 1
ACADABIL: 2 2 39 2 1 1 4 0 1 2 1  5 1 2 2 2 2 2 3 1 1 2 1 2 2 2 1  6 1  7 1 2 2
RACE: 1 2 2 4 2 1 1 2 2
ACADABIL: 2 2 20 1 1 2 2 1 2 2 1 20 2 2 1 2 2 2 2 2 1 2 1 1 2 1 4  6 1  7 1 2 2
RACE: 1 2 2 3 2 1 2 2 0
ACADABIL: 1 2 18 1 1 4 1 0 2 1 2  5 3 2 2 2 1 2 5 1 1 2 1 3 2 3 2 13 6 12 2 3 2
RACE: 1 2 3 3 1 2 1 1 4
ACADABIL: 2 2 19 1 1 2 1 0 1 1 1 20 2 2 2 2 2 2 1 1 1 2 2 1 2 2 2  5 3  5 0 1 2
RACE: 1 2 1 4 2 1 1 2 0
ACADABIL: 2 2 18 2 1 2 1 0 2 2 1  1 2 2 2 2 2 2 1 1 1 2 2 2 3 3  5 1  8 1 2 2
RACE: 1 2 2 3 2 1 1 2 1
ACADABIL: 2 2 21 1 1 4 3 0 2 1 4 10 3 2 2 2 2 4 1 2 2 1 3 2 2 1 16 3 13 3 3 2
RACE: 1 2 4 3 1 4 1 2 2
ACADABIL: 2 2 21 2 1 2 3 2 1 1 1  3 1 2 1 2 2 2 2 1 1 2 2 1 2 4 2  6 2  4 0 1 1
RACE: 1 2 1 2 2 1 1 2 1
ACADABIL: 2 2 20 2 1 3 2 0 2 2 1 40 1 1 2 2 2 2 1 1 1 2 2 2 2 4 2  6 0  5 1 1 2
RACE: 1 2 1 4 2 1 2 2 1
ACADABIL: 2 2 18 2 1 2 1 0 1 2 1  2 1 2 2 2 2 2 2 1 1 2 2 1 2 1 1  6 0  4 0 1 2
RACE: 1 2 1 4 2 1 2 2 1
ACADABIL: 2 2 21 1 1 3 3 2 2 1 1 10 2 2 2 2 2 1 3 1 2 2 1 3 1 2 1  9 3  9 3 2 2
RACE: 1 2 2 3 1 2 1 2 2
ACADABIL: 2 2 18 2 1 1 1 2 1 2 1 55 1 4 1 2 2 2 1 1 2 2 2 2 1 0 2  4 0  5 1 1 2
RACE: 1 2 1 1 1 1 2 2 0
ACADABIL: 2 2 21 2 1 2 3 0 1 2 1 10 1 2 2 2 2 2 1 1 1 2 2 2 2 4 1  5 0  6 0 1 2
RACE: 1 2 2 2 2 1 2 2 2
ACADABIL: 2 2 18 2 1 1 1 0 1 2 1 10 1 1 2 2 2 2 1 1 1 2 2 1 2 3 1  4 0  4 0 1 2
RACE: 1 2 1 3 2 1 2 2 0
ACADABIL: 2 2 19 2 1 1 2 0 1 2 1  5 1 2 2 2 2 2 1 1 2 2 2 1 2 0 1  4 0  4 1 1 2
```

```
RACE: 1 2 1 3 2 1 2 2 0

ACADABIL: 2 2 20 2 1 2 3 0 1 2 1 20 1 2 1 2 2 2 2 1 2 2 2 1 2 1 1   6 0   5 1 1 2
    RACE: 1 2 2 4 2 1 2 2 1

ACADABIL: 2 2 21 2 1 2 3 0 1 2 1   5 1 2 2 2 2 2 2 1 2 2 2 1 2 4 1   6 1   5 1 1 2
    RACE: 1 2 2 3 2 1 1 2 1

ACADABIL: 2 2 18 2 1 2 1 0 1 2 1   8 1 2 2 2 2 2 1 1 1 2 2 3 2 1 1   5 0   7 0 1 2
    RACE: 1 2 2 3 1 1 2 2 0

ACADABIL: 1 2 22 1 1 2 4 0 1 1 2 20 2 4 2 2 1 2 3 2 1 2 2 2 2 3 4   9 5  11 0 4 2
    RACE: 1 2 3 1 1 2 1 2 2

ACADABIL: 2 2 22 2 1 2 4 0 1 1 1 10 1 5 2 2 2 2 1 2 1 2 2 1 2 3 4   5 1   4 0 1 2
    RACE: 1 2 1 3 2 1 2 2 1

ACADABIL: 2 2 20 1 1 1 1 1 1 1 1 99 1 2 1 2 2 2 1 2 1 2 2 1 2 2 4   4 3   4 0 1 2
    RACE: 1 2 1 1 2 1 1 2 0

ACADABIL: 1 2 19 1 1 2 2 0 1 1 2 10 1 1 2 2 2 2 2 1 1 2 2 1 2 3 2   8 4   6 0 2 2
    RACE: 1 2 2 3 2 2 2 1 2

ACADABIL: 2 2 20 2 1 2 2 0 2 2 2 75 2 2 2 2 2 2 2 1 1 2 2 3 2 2 4   8 0  11 1 3 2
    RACE: 1 2 3 3 2 2 2 2 1

ACADABIL: 2 2 20 2 1 2 2 0 2 2 1 40 1 2 2 2 2 1 1 1 1 1 1 2 2 3   5 1   5 3 1 2
    RACE: 1 2 2 3 2 1 1 2 2

ACADABIL: 2 2 19 2 1 3 2 1 1 2 1 10 1 2 1 2 2 2 1 1 1 2 2 4 2 0 4   6 1  11 0 2 2
    RACE: 1 2 4 4 2 1 1 2 0

ACADABIL: 2 1 21 1 1 3 3 1 2 2 1   4 2 5 2 2 2 2 3 1 1 2 2 1 2 2 2   9 1   7 1 2 2
    RACE: 1 2 2 4 1 2 2 2 2

ACADABIL: 2 2 18 2 1 2 1 0 1 2 1   7 1 2 2 2 2 2 2 1 1 2 2 1 2 3 1   6 0   5 0 1 2
    RACE: 1 2 2 3 2 1 2 2 2

ACADABIL: 2 2 20 2 1 1 2 0 1 2 1 40 1 1 2 2 2 2 1 1 1 2 2 1 2 1 3   4 1   4 0 1 2
    RACE: 1 2 1 4 2 1 1 2 1

ACADABIL: 2 1 20 1 1 1 2 1 1 1 1   5 1 2 2 2 2 2 2 1 1 2 2 1 2 1 1   5 2   5 0 1 2
    RACE: 1 2 2 3 2 1 2 2 1

ACADABIL: 2 2 21 1 1 3 4 0 1 1 1   5 2 5 2 2 2 2 3 1 1 2 1 2 2 0 4   8 3   7 1 1 2
    RACE: 1 2 2 2 2 1 2 1 0

ACADABIL: 2 2 19 2 1 1 1 0 1 2 1 20 2 2 2 2 2 2 2 2 1 2 2 2 2 2 3 4   5 0   6 1 1 2
    RACE: 1ʳ 2 1 3 2 1 2 2 1

ACADABIL: 1 2 19 1 1 2 1 0 1 1 1 10 2 2 2 2 1 2 1 1 2 2 2 1 2 4 1   5 6   6 1 1 2
    RACE: 1 2 2 3 2 1 1 1 2

ACADABIL: 2 2 19 2 1 2 2 0 1 2 1   5 3 2 2 2 2 2 2 1 2 2 2 3 2 0 1   6 0  10 1 2 2
```

```
RACE:  1 2 2 4 2 1 2 2 0

ACADABIL: 1 2 22 1 1 4 4 0 1 1 1 99 1 2 2 2 2 2 1 3 1 2 1 2 2 2 3 11 4   7 1 1 2
    RACE:  3 2 3 4 2 5 1 2 0

ACADABIL: 2 2 19 2 1 2 2 0 2 2 2 10 2 2 2 2 2 2 2 2 1 2 2 2 2 0 2  8 0   8 1 2 2
    RACE:  1 2 2 3 2 2 2 2 1

ACADABIL: 2 2 18 1 1 1 1 0 2 2 1 25 1 5 2 2 2 2 3 2 1 2 2 1 2 3 1   7 2   7 1 3 2
    RACE:  1 2 2 1 2 2 1 2 3

ACADABIL: 1 2 19 2 1 3 1 1 1 1 2 30 1 4 1 2 2 2 4 2 2 2 2 2 2 5 1 13 3   6 1 1 2
    RACE:  1 2 2 3 2 4 2 1 3

ACADABIL: 2 2 21 2 1 3 2 0 1 2 2  3 2 2 2 2 2 2 2 1 1 2 2 2 2 2 4 11 0   8 0 2 2
    RACE:  1 2 2 3 1 4 2 2 1

ACADABIL: 1 2 20 1 1 4 4 0 2 1 1  2 4 1 2 2 2 2 3 1 2 1 1 4 2 4 1 13 5 15 4 4 2
    RACE:  1 2 3 4 1 5 1 1 4

ACADABIL: 2 2 21 1 1 2 3 0 2 1 1  1 2 2 2 2 2 2 1 1 2 2 1 2 2 3 1   7 3   8 3 2 2
    RACE:  1 2 2 4 1 3 1 2 2

ACADABIL: 2 2 18 2 1 2 1 0 1 2 1 10 2 2 2 2 2 2 1 2 1 2 2 1 2 0 2   5 1   6 0 1 2
    RACE:  1 2 2 3 1 1 1 2 0

ACADABIL: 2 2 18 2 1 2 2 0 1 2 1 15 2 5 2 2 2 2 1 2 1 2 2 1 2 2 3   5 1   6 0 1 2
    RACE:  1 2 2 2 1 1 1 2 1

ACADABIL: 2 2 21 2 1 1 4 2 1 2 1 10 1 5 1 1 2 2 1 2 2 2 2 1 2 2 2   4 1   4 1 1 2
    RACE:  1 2 1 3 2 1 1 2 0

ACADABIL: 2 2 18 1 1 1 1 0 1 1 1  5 2 1 2 2 2 2 1 2 1 2 2 2 2 2 2   4 3   8 0 2 2
    RACE:  1 2 2 4 1 1 1 2 1

ACADABIL: 2 2 19 2 1 2 2 0 1 2 1  1 2 2 2 2 2 2 3 1 1 2 2 2 2 2 1   8 0   6 0 1 2
    RACE:  1 2 1 3 2 2 2 2 2

ACADABIL: 2 2 19 2 1 1 1 0 2 2 1 40 3 2 2 2 2 2 3 1 1 2 1 2 2 1 4   6 1   9 2 2 2
    RACE:  1 2 2 3 1 1 1 2 0

ACADABIL: 1 2 21 1 1 3 3 0 2 1 5 85 4 2 2 2 1 2 2 1 1 1 1 3 2 3 1 14 6 13 2 3 2
    RACE:  1 2 3 3 1 4 1 1 3

ACADABIL: 1 2 21 1 1 3 3 0 2 1 2  0 4 1 2 2 1 2 4 1 1 2 1 1 2 4 1 11 5 13 2 4 2
    RACE:  1 2 4 4 1 2 2 1 4

ACADABIL: 2 2 18 2 1 1 1 0 2 2 1 30 2 2 2 2 2 2 3 1 2 2 2 2 2 . 1   6 0   7 2 1 2
    RACE:  1 2 2 1 2 1 2 2 .

ACADABIL: 2 2 20 2 1 3 1 0 1 2 1 50 1 4 2 2 2 2 3 2 1 2 1 1 2 3 4   8 0   4 1 1 2
    RACE:  3 2 1 2 2 1 2 2 1

ACADABIL: 2 2 22 1 1 2 4 0 1 2 1  2 1 2 2 2 2 2 2 1 1 2 2 1 2 0 1   6 2   6 0 2 2
```

```
        RACE:  1  2  2  3  1  1  1  2  0

ACADABIL: 2  2 36  2  1  2  3  1  1  2  1   3  1  2  1  2  2  2  2  1  2  2  2  1  2  0  1    6  1    6  1  2  2
        RACE:  1  2  2  4  2  1  1  2  0

ACADABIL: 2  2 19  2  1  3  2  0  2  2  1  20  2  2  2  2  2  2  3  1  2  2  2  2  2  2  1 10  1    8  2  2  2
        RACE:  1  2  2  4  1  3  1  2  1

ACADABIL: 2  1    .  2  1  1  1  3  1  1  1  20  1  2  1  2  1  2  3  1  1  2  1  1  2  2  1    6  2    4  1  1  2
        RACE:  1  1  1  3  1  1  2  2  1

ACADABIL: 2  2 20  1  1  3  3  0  1  1  1   5  1  2  2  2  2  2  2  1  2  2  2  1  2  5  2    7  6    6  1  2  2
        RACE:  1  2  2  3  2  1  1  2  3

ACADABIL: 2  2 35  2  1  2  3  1  1  2  1   5  1  2  1  2  2  2  2  1  1  2  2  1  2  4  1    6  0    4  0  1  2
        RACE:  1  2  1  3  2  1  2  2  1

ACADABIL: 1  2 21  1  1  4  3  0  2  1  1   1  2  1  2  2  1  2  5  1  2  1  1  1  2  1  1  11  6 10  4  3  2
        RACE:  1  2  4  4  1  1  1  1  4

ACADABIL: 1  2 18  1  1  3  1  0  2  1  3  10  2  2  2  2  1  2  5  1  2  1  1  2  2  3  1 14  6    7  4  1  2
        RACE:  1  2  2  2  1  3  1  1  4

ACADABIL: 2  2 18  2  1  5  1  0  1  2  5  25  4  4  2  2  2  2  5  1  1  2  2  4  2  3  1 25  0 14  0  3  2
        RACE:  1  2  3  3  1  5  2  2  0

ACADABIL: 2  2 20  2  1  2  2  0  2  2  1  40  2  2  2  2  2  2  3  1  2  1  1  3  2  2  1    8  1 11  2  2  2
        RACE:  1  2  4  3  1  2  1  2  1

ACADABIL: 2  2 20  1  1  2  2  0  2  2  1   5  2  2  2  2  2  2  2  1  1  2  2  2  2  2  1    6  1    9  1  2  2
        RACE:  1  2  3  3  1  1  2  2  1

ACADABIL: 1  1 21  1  1  4  3  2  2  1  4   0  3  2  2  2  1  2  1  1  2  2  1  3  2  0  1  13  6 12  3  3  2
        RACE:  1  1  3  3  1  4  1  1  5

ACADABIL: 2  2 21  1  1  3  4  0  2  1  1   3  1  2  2  2  2  2  3  1  1  2  2  3  2  3  1    8  3 10  1  2  2
        RACE:  1  2  4  3  2  1  1  2  2

ACADABIL: 1  2 19  2  1  3  2  0  2  1  2   0  2  2  2  2  1  2  2  1  1  1  2  2  2  1  1    9  3    9  2  2  2
        RACE:  1  2  3  3  2  2  2  2  1

ACADABIL: 1  2 18  1  1  5  1  0  1  1  3  10  4  2  2  2  1  2  5  1  1  2  2  4  2  3  4  17  6 15  4  4  2
        RACE:  1  2  3  3  1  4  1  1  4

ACADABIL: 2  2 20  2  1  3  1  0  1  2  1   1  1  2  2  2  2  1  1  1  2  2  1  2  3  2    6  0    4  0  1  2
        RACE:  1  2  1  3  1  1  2  2  0

ACADABIL: 2  2 28  2  1  2  4  0  1  2  1  20  1  1  2  2  2  2  1  1  1  2  1  1  2  3  4    8  0    6  1  2  2
        RACE:  1  2  2  2  1  4  2  2  1

ACADABIL: 2  2 18  2  1  2  1  0  2  2  1   5  2  5  2  2  2  2  1  1  1  2  2  2  2  4  2    6  1    7  1  1  2
        RACE:  1  2  2  2  2  1  2  2

ACADABIL: 2  2 19  2  1  1  1  0  2  2  1  10  2  2  2  2  2  2  1  1  1  2  2  2  2  2  1    4  0    7  1  2  2
```

```
          RACE: 1 2 1 2 1 1 2 2 1
      ACADABIL: 1 2 19 1 1 5 1 0 1 1 3 10 3 2 2 2 1 2 5 1 1 1 1 3 2 1 1 16 6 10 2 2 2
          RACE: 1 2 2 1 1 3 1 1 1
      ACADABIL: 2 2 18 1 1 2 1 0 2 1 1 10 3 2 2 2 2 3 1 2 2 1 4 2 2 1  9 2 11 3 2 2
          RACE: 1 2 2 1 1 3 2 2 1
      ACADABIL: 1 2 19 2 1 3 1 0 2 2 2  5 3 2 2 2 1 2 4 1 2 2 1 3 2 . 1 12 3 10 3 2 2
          RACE: 1 2 2 3 1 3 2 1 3
      ACADABIL: 2 2 19 1 1 2 1 0 2 1 1  5 2 2 2 2 2 2 3 1 2 2 2 2 2 4  7 3  9 2 2 2
          RACE: 1 2 3 2 1 1 1 2 1
      ACADABIL: 2 2 20 2 1 3 3 0 2 2 1  1 2 1 2 2 2 2 2 1 1 2 2 2 2 4 4  7 0  8 1 2 2
          RACE: 1 2 2 4 2 1 2 2 2
      ACADABIL: 2 2 20 2 1 2 3 0 1 2 1 10 1 2 2 2 2 2 4 1 2 2 2 2 2 0 4  8 0  7 1 2 2
          RACE: 1 2 2 3 2 1 2 2 0
      ACADABIL: 2 2 18 2 1 1 1 0 1 2 1 90 1 2 2 2 2 2 1 3 1 2 2 1 2 0 2  4 1  4 0 1 2
          RACE: 2 2 1 3 2 1 1 2 0
      ACADABIL: 2 2 18 2 1 3 1 0 1 1 1 25 2 2 2 2 2 2 5 1 2 2 2 2 3 2 10 2 10 1 3 2
          RACE: 1 2 3 3 2 1 2 1 3
      ACADABIL: 2 2 18 2 1 2 1 0 2 1 1  2 1 2 2 2 2 2 1 2 2 2 1 1 2 2 3  5 2  5 3 1 2
          RACE: 1 2 2 4 2 1 1 2 2
      ACADABIL: 2 2 21 2 1 3 2 0 1 2 1  5 2 2 2 2 2 2 2 1 2 2 2 2 2 4  9 0  8 1 2 2
          RACE: 1 2 2 3 1 3 2 2 1
      ACADABIL: 2 2 18 2 1 2 1 0 2 2 1 15 1 2 2 2 2 2 3 1 1 2 1 1 2 1 4  7 1  5 1 1 2
          RACE: 1 2 2 3 2 1 1 2 0
      ACADABIL: 2 2 19 2 1 3 1 0 1 2 1 40 2 2 2 2 2 2 2 2 2 1 3 2 1 1  7 1  9 2 2 2
          RACE: 1 2 2 3 1 1 1 2 1
      ACADABIL: 2 2 18 2 1 5 1 0 1 2 5 98 1 2 2 2 2 2 5 3 1 2 1 1 2 4 2 20 0  4 1 1 2
          RACE: 2 2 1 3 2 5 2 2 1
      ACADABIL: 2 2 18 2 1 2 1 0 1 2 2 40 2 2 2 2 2 2 1 1 2 2 2 2 4 2  5 1  7 1 1 2
          RACE: 1 2 2 4 2 1 1 2 1
      ACADABIL: 2 2 19 2 1 3 1 0 1 2 1  . 2 1 2 2 2 2 3 1 1 2 2 2 2 3 1  8 0  8 0 2 2
          RACE: 1 2 2 3 2 1 2 2 1
      ACADABIL: 2 2 19 2 1 2 1 0 2 1 1 10 1 5 2 2 2 2 1 1 1 2 2 1 2 1 3  5 2  4 1 1 2
          RACE: 1 2 1 4 2 1 1 2 0
      ACADABIL: 2 2 20 1 1 4 3 0 2 2 5 95 3 1 2 2 2 2 4 1 1 2 1 3 2 4 4 18 1 12 2 3 2
          RACE: 1 2 3 3 2 5 1 2 2
      ACADABIL: 2 2 19 2 1 2 1 0 1 2 1  5 2 2 2 2 2 2 1 1 1 2 2 2 2 0 2  5 0  9 0 3 2
```

```
RACE: 1 2 2 3 1 1 2 2 0

ACADABIL: 2 2 18 1 1 3 1 0 1 1 4 20 1 2 2 2 2 2 2 2 2 1 2 2 2 3 10 3  8 2 1 2
   RACE: 1 2 4 2 1 1 1 2 1

ACADABIL: 2 2 20 2 1 3 3 0 2 2 1  1 2 1 2 2 2 2 2 1 2 2 1 2 2 3 1  7 0  8 3 2 2
   RACE: 1 2 2 4 2 1 2 2 2

ACADABIL: 2 2 20 2 1 2 3 0 1 2 1 25 2 1 2 2 2 2 2 1 2 2 2 2 2 4  6 1  6 1 1 2
   RACE: 1 2 1 4 2 1 1 2 0

ACADABIL: 2 1 18 2 1 2 1 1 1 2 1 98 2 2 2 2 2 2 1 1 1 2 2 2 3 1  5 0  8 0 2 2
   RACE: 1 2 2 4 1 1 2 2 0

ACADABIL: 2 2 23 2 1 1 4 0 2 2 1 15 1 5 2 2 1 2 1 2 1 2 2 1 2 2 4  6 1  6 1 2 2
   RACE: 1 2 2 2 1 3 2 2 1

ACADABIL: 2 2 23 2 1 1 3 0 1 2 1 60 2 2 2 2 2 2 3 2 2 2 2 2 0 2 10 1  6 1 1 2
   RACE: 5 2 1 2 1 5 1 2 0

ACADABIL: 2 2 19 2 1 2 2 0 2 2 1 30 1 5 2 2 2 2 3 2 2 2 2 1 2 1 1  8 0  4 2 1 2
   RACE: 5 2 1 3 1 2 2 2 0

ACADABIL: 2 2 19 1 1 2 1 0 2 2 1 10 1 2 2 2 2 2 1 1 1 2 1 3 2 2 1  5 1  8 2 2 2
   RACE: 1 2 2 4 2 1 2 2 0

ACADABIL: 1 2 19 1 1 3 2 0 2 1 1  1 1 2 2 2 1 2 5 1 1 1 1 1 2 4 1 10 5  6 3 2 2
   RACE: 1 2 2 3 2 1 2 1 4

ACADABIL: 2 2 19 2 1 2 2 0 1 2 1 60 1 5 2 2 2 2 2 1 2 2 1 2 3 2  6 0  4 2 1 2
   RACE: 1 2 1 2 1 1 2 2 1

ACADABIL: 2 2 18 2 1 1 1 0 2 2 1 20 1 2 2 2 2 2 1 1 1 2 2 2 2 1 2  4 0  5 1 1 2
   RACE: 1 2 1 4 2 1 2 2 1

ACADABIL: 2 2 18 2 1 1 1 0 1 2 1 20 1 2 2 2 2 2 2 1 2 2 2 1 2 0 3  8 1  4 1 1 2
   RACE: 1 2 1 2 1 4 1 2 0

ACADABIL: 2 1 25 2 1 1 4 1 2 2 1 35 1 2 2 2 2 2 1 1 1 2 2 2 2 2 3  4 1  6 1 1 2
   RACE: 1 2 2 3 1 1 1 2 1

ACADABIL: 2 2 21 2 1 1 3 0 2 1 1 30 1 1 2 2 2 2 1 1 1 2 1 1 2 3 1  4 2  4 2 1 2
   RACE: 1 2 1 4 1 1 1 2 1

ACADABIL: 2 1 18 2 1 1 1 1 1 2 1  7 1 2 2 2 2 2 1 1 1 2 2 1 2 3 4  4 0  4 0 1 2
   RACE: 1 2 1 3 2 1 2 2 1

ACADABIL: 2 1 18 1 1 3 1 1 1 1 1 10 1 4 2 2 2 2 1 2 1 2 1 1 2 0 3  6 3  4 1 1 2
   RACE: 2 2 1 2 1 2 1 0

ACADABIL: 2 2 18 2 1 5 1 0 2 1 5 50 1 4 2 2 2 2 5 1 1 2 2 1 2 3 2 20 2  5 1 1 2
   RACE: 1 2 2 2 5 1 2 0

ACADABIL: 2 2 19 2 1 2 1 0 2 2 1 90 2 1 2 2 2 2 1 1 2 1 1 2 2 2 4  5 0  8 0 2 2
```

```
RACE: 1 2 2 3 2 1 2 2 0
ACADABIL: 1 2 20 2 1 1 3 0 1 1 1 40 2 1 2 2 2 2 3 1 1 2 2 3 2 4 3  8 2  9 0 2 2
    RACE: 1 2 2 1 1 3 2 2 1
ACADABIL: 2 2 18 1 1 2 1 0 1 1 1 10 1 5 2 2 2 2 1 1 2 2 2 1 2 0 2  5 2  4 1 1 2
    RACE: 2 2 1 2 2 1 2 2 0
ACADABIL: 2 2 18 2 1 2 1 0 1 1 1 98 1 5 2 2 2 2 5 1 2 2 2 1 2 2 2 10 1  4 1 1 2
    RACE: 2 2 1 1 2 2 2 2 2
ACADABIL: 2 2 19 2 1 1 1 0 2 2 1 25 1 2 2 2 2 2 1 1 1 2 2 3 2 2 1  4 0  7 1 1 2
    RACE: 1 2 2 2 2 1 2 2 0
ACADABIL: 1 2 18 1 1 4 1 0 2 1 3  0 2 2 2 2 1 2 4 2 1 2 1 2 2 1 2 14 5  9 2 2 2
    RACE: 1 2 3 2 1 3 2 1 2
ACADABIL: 1 2 20 1 1 2 1 0 2 1 2  1 2 2 2 2 2 2 4 1 2 2 1 3 2 1 4 11 4 11 3 4 2
    RACE: 1 2 2 2 1 3 2 1 1
ACADABIL: 2 2 20 2 1 1 2 0 1 2 1 25 1 2 2 2 2 2 1 2 1 2 2 1 2 3 1  4 0  4 0 1 2
    RACE: 1 2 1 2 1 1 2 2 0
ACADABIL: 2 2 21 2 1 1 4 1 1 2 1 30 1 2 2 1 2 2 3 1 1 2 2 1 2 4 2  7 0  4 0 1 2
    RACE: 1 2 1 3 2 1 2 2 2
ACADABIL: 2 2 20 2 1 1 3 0 2 1 1 25 1 2 2 2 2 2 2 1 1 2 2 1 2 3 2  5 2  4 1 1 2
    RACE: 1 2 1 3 1 1 1 2 0
ACADABIL: 2 2 20 1 1 3 2 0 1 2 1  2 1 2 2 2 2 2 2 1 1 2 2 1 2 3 2  7 2  4 0 1 2
    RACE: 1 2 1 3 1 1 1 2 2

Number of cases read:  136    Number of cases listed:  136
```

BIBLIOGRAPHY

Babbie, Earl. 1990. "The Essential Wisdom of Sociology." *Teaching Sociology* 18:526-530.

Babbie, Earl. 1995. *The Practice of Social Research.* Seventh Edition. Belmont, California: Wadsworth Publishing Company.

Ballantine, Jeanne. 1991. "Market Needs and Program Products: The Articulation Between Undergraduate Applied Programs and the Market Place." *Journal of Applied Sociology* 8:1-18.

Becker, Howard S. 1986. *Writing for Social Scientists: How to Start and Finish Your Thesis, Book, or Article.* Chicago: University of Chicago Press.

Bennett, William J. 1994. *The Index of Leading Cultural Indicators.* New York: Simon & Schuster.

Berenson, Mark L.; David M. Levine and David Rindskopf. 1988. *Applied Statistics.* Englewood Cliffs, New Jersey: Prentice Hall.

Blalock, Hubert M., Jr. 1979. *Social Statistics.* New York: McGraw-Hill.

Davis, James A. 1992. *General Social Surveys: Cumulative Codebook.* Conducted for the National Data Program for the Social Sciences at National Opinion Research Center, University of Chicago. Storrs, Connecticut: Roper Center for Public Opinion Research.

Fischer, Henry W., III. 1993. *Social Statistics, the IBM-PC and SPSS/PC+*. Teaching Resources Series. Washington, D.C.: American Sociological Association.

Fischer, Henry W., III. 1994. *Response to Disaster: Fact Versus Fiction & Its Perpetuation. The Sociology of Disaster*. Lanham, Maryland: University Press of America.

Fischer, Henry W., III. 1996. "Teaching Statistics From the User's Perspective." *Teaching Sociology* 24:225-230.

Gore, Albert. 1993. *The Gore Report on Reinventing Government*. New York: Times Books.

Hamilton, Lawrence C. 1996. *Data Analysis for Social Scientists*. Belmont, California: Wadsworth Publishing Company.

Hoover, Kenneth R. 1992. *The Elements of Social Scientific Thinking*. Fifth Edition. New York: St. Martin's Press.

Katzer, Jeffrey; Kenneth H. Cook and Wayne W. Crouch. 1991. *Evaluating Information: A Guide for Users of Social Science Research. Third Edition. New York: McGraw-Hill, Inc.*

Krause, Daniel. 1996. *Effective Program Evaluation*. Chicago: Nelson-Hall Publishers.

Lake, Celinda C. 1987. *Public Opinion Polling*. Washington, D.C.: Island Press.

Lee, Ivy and Minako Maykovich. 1995. *Statistics: A Tool for Understanding Society*. Boston: Allyn and Bacon.

Loether, Herman J. and Donald G. McTavish. 1993. *Descriptive and Inferential Statistics*. Fourth Edition. Boston: Allyn and Bacon.

Maier, Mark H. 1991. *The Data Game: Controversies in Social Science Statistics*. Armonk, New York: M.E. Sharpe, Inc.

May, Tim. 1993. *Social Research: Issues, Methods and Process*. Philadelphia: Open University Press.

Moore, David S. and George P. McCabe. 1993. *Introduction to the Practice of Statistics*. New York: Freeman and Company.

Norusis, Marija J. and SPSS Inc. 1995. *SPSS for Windows: Base System User's Guide. Release 7.0*. Chicago, Illinois: SPSS Inc.

Richlin-Klonsky, Judith and Ellen Strenski (eds.). 1994. *A Guide to Writing Sociology Papers*. Third Edition. New York: St. Martin's Press.

Rosnow, Ralph L. and Robert Rosenthal. 1993. *Beginning Behavioral Research*. New York: Macmillan Publishing Company.

Scarpitti, Frank R. and F. Kurt Cylke, Jr. 1995. *Social Problems: The Search for Solutions*. Los Angeles, California: Roxbury Publishing Company.

Spatz, Chris. 1993. *Basic Statistics*. Fifth Edition. Pacific Grove, California: Brooks and Cole Publishing Company.

Steele, Stephen F. and E. Joseph Lamp. 1987. *Establishing College and University Local Research Centers.* Washington, D.C.: The American Sociological Association Teaching Resource Program.

Steele, Stephen F. 1994. "The Craft of Applied Sociology: Skills, Challenges, and Vision." *Journal of Applied Sociology* 11:1-10.

Sullivan, Thomas J. 1992. *Applied Sociology: Research and Critical Thinking.* New York: Macmillan Publishing Company.

Wallace, Walter L. 1971. *The Logic of Science in Sociology.* New York: Aldine Publishing Company.

Weiss, Gregory L. 1986. *The Roanoke Valley Poll.* Roanoke, Virginia: The Center for Community Research, Roanoke College.

KEY WORK INDEX

ABOUT THE AUTHOR

Henry W. Fischer, III holds a Ph.D. in sociology which he completed at the University of Delaware in 1986. He has had articles published in several refereed scholarly journals which focus on teaching sociology and which focus on the behavioral and organizational response to disaster (his primary research interest). In 1993 the American Sociological Association published his book *Social Statistics, the IBM-PC, and SPSS-PC+: A Manual for the User* as part of its Teaching Resource Series. In 1994 University Press of America published his book *Response to Disaster: Fact Versus Fiction & Its Perpetuation--the Sociology of Disaster* which has received very positive book reviews. Dr. Fischer currently directs the Social Research Group (SRG) at Millersville University of Pennsylvania. Millersville is one of fourteen campuses which comprise the Pennsylvania System of Higher Education. He is an active member of the International Research Committee on Disasters, the American Sociological Association, the Society for Applied Sociology, the Eastern Sociological Society, and the Pennsylvania Sociological Society. He can be reached at his office via 717-872-3568, FAX 717-871-2429, e-mail *hfischer@marauder.millersv.edu*.